CONCILIUM

concilium

1991/4

NO HEAVEN WITHOUT EARTH

Edited by

**Johann Baptist Metz and
Edward Schillebeeckx**

SCM Press · London

Trinity Press International · Philadelphia

August 1991

ISBN: 0334 03009 9

Typeset at The Spartan Press Ltd, Lymington, Hants
Printed by Dotesios Ltd, Trowbridge, Wilts

Concilium: Published February, April, June, August, October, December.

For the best and promptest service, new subscribers should apply as follows:

US and Canadian subscribers:

Trinity Press International, 3725 Chestnut Street, Philadelphia PA 19104
Fax: 215–387–8805

UK and other subscribers:

SCM Press, 26–30 Tottenham Road, London N1 4BZ
Fax: 071–249 3776

Existing subscribers should direct any queries about their subscriptions as above.

Subscription rates are as follows:
United States and Canada: US$59.95
United Kingdom, Europe, the rest of the world (surface): £34.95
Airmail to countries outside Europe: £44.95

Further copies of this issue and copies of most back issues of *Concilium* are available at US$12.95 (US and Canada)/£6.95 rest of the world.

Contents

Editorial

This issue of *Concilium* centres on the theme of theology and ecology. Its main intention is to work out the substantive theological and ecclesiological significance of this theme. So it is not about futurology, nor is it concerned with scientific or sociological analyses: it is about theology, but theology which seeks to take account of the non-theological scientific criteria in this question. The focal point of the issue is ecology: both ecology related to nature and social ecology. The individual contributions seek to open up the whole breadth of this complex of problems from the perspectives of *krisis* and *kairos*.

It is often said that the problems connected with this theme have nothing to do with the heart of the gospel and the vision of the kingdom of God. This volume seeks to make it clear that preoccupation with these questions is not just an ethical obligation for the church which arises in the course of its history but one that stems from the very foundation of its task. This preoccupation is incumbent on the church as the church of Jesus Christ. The commitment to justice, peace and the integrity of creation extends to the foundations of the church's identity. 'No heaven without earth!' So church life is inseparably bound up with the process of this earthly life. Once again, this issue seeks to demonstrate that faith and the community of the church do not exist beyond this world, but that they are an expression of this world as it originates from God and turns and returns to God.

Unfortunately one article in the first part, which is concerned with the way in which God brings about redemption through intermediaries in the cosmos and history, failed to materialize. It was to have dealt with the significance of the earth from the perspective of the theology of creation and eschatology. Fortunately, in the first article Johan de Tavernier deals with the problem of mediation between the eschatological kingdom of God and our present world, between eschatological hope and our action in the world. In this context he produces criteria for interpreting the 'secular' course of history as a history of salvation or its opposite.

The second group of themes, explicitly concentrated on the 'conciliar process', offers an extended critique by René Coste of the ecumenical assemblies in Basle (1989) and Seoul (1990) – above all in connection with the questions which relate to our theme. Anton van Harskamp discusses the disputed terms 'conciliar', 'conciliar process', and on the basis of his findings seeks to work out and rescue the substance of an authoritative statement by the church communities on the unity of humankind.

Central issues relating to theology and ecology are discussed in the third group of themes. Alexandre Ganoczy's concern is to discover (or rediscover) starting points for an ecological ethics from the Christian tradition – biblical and patristic theology, mediaeval piety, the Second Vatican Council – which might be usefully adopted in contemporary discussion. In the light of a comprehensive understanding of creation Günter Altner understands human beings to be responsible for an ethic which also includes the non-human creation; he formulates principles and rules for responsible human action and calls for the codification of rights for nature and for future generations. Johan van Klinken is concerned with ecological questions at the interface between theology and the natural sciences, especially with a non-anthropocentric understanding of creation in which human beings are seen as 'stewards' who take care of creation and are in a covenant relationship with it. In discussing what Hans Jonas calls the 'principle of responsibility' and what are known as the 'ethics of discourse', Werner Kroh brings out the central content and limitations of these two positions, whhich have become very influential in the discussion of a fundamental 'ecological ethic'. In doing so he shows the significance of anamnetic reason for a communicative ethics in which responsibility for the future of humankind is formulated. In his plea for 'ecological wisdom' in Christianity, John Carmody attempts to overcome the objections, rooted in biblical monotheism, to a mythologizing of nature and history and to move towards a new 'mythical relationship to nature'.

Roger Burggraeve's concluding article is based on the biblical vision of the new heaven and the new earth. He stresses that dealing with the world as a 'gift of God' is one of the premises and not one of the results of human freedom. So the world as creation is not at the disposal of an anthropology of domination.

All the articles in this issue are ultimately aimed at so linking worldly commitment and the prophetic criticism of faith that our world is not forced below the level of God's creation.

Edward Schillebeeckx
Johann Baptist Metz

Centesimus Annus: Who Got the Stronger Penance?

A cartoon in the American newspaper *The National Catholic Reporter* tried to capture, in one vivid image, the gist of the new encyclical. The Pope is shown seated in a confession box hearing the confessions of two penitents kneeling on either side of his confessional. The cartoon labelled one of the penitents as capitalism, the other as socialism. Without doubt, *Centesimus Annus* proclaims the sins (not mere *peccadillos*) of both economic systems.

Socialism is condemned for its fundamental anthropological error. 'Man is reduced to a series of social relationships, and the concept of the person as the autonomous subject of moral decision disappears' (13). Socialism also comes in for condemnation because of the doctrine of the class struggle (14) and the inefficiency of its economic system as a consequence of the violation of the human rights to private initiative, to ownership of property and to freedom in the economic sector (24). Rather strangely, however, the encyclical somewhat carelessly conflates the two terms socialism and what is termed 'real socialism', i.e. the state capitalism of the Eastern bloc countries. What is being proposed as an alternative is not the socalist system which in fact turns out to be state capitalism, but rather a society of free work, of enterprise and of participation (35). In actual fact, of course, there exist varieties of market socialism.

Concerning capitalism, the Pope notes how, to a large extent, the condemnations of *Rerum Novarum* against primitive capitalism still ring true today. 'In spite of the great changes which have taken place in the more advanced societies, the human inadequacies of capitalism and the resulting domination of things over people are far from disappearing' (33). In the Third World, especially, in a world capitalist market, 'the fact is that many people, perhaps the majority today, do not have the means which would enable them to take their place in an effective and humanly dignified way within a productive system in which work is truly central' (33). Capitalism receives censure for the consumerism it promotes and the latent risk, in its mechanisms, of 'an idolatry of the market, an idolatry which ignores the existence of goods which by their nature are not and cannot be mere commodities' (40). Real capitalism includes alienation, alienation from authentic work and the loss of the deepest meaning of life (41). Hence, the Pope concludes that, 'We have seen that it is unacceptable to say that the defeat of so-called "Real-Socialism" leaves capitalism as the only model of economic organization' (35).

As with every social encyclical, the reception of this new teaching has been quite varied. *Le Monde* reacted by stressing its anti-capitalist tone. *The Wall Street Journal* and *The Washington Post* placed major emphasis on the pro-capitalist motifs. Which of the penitents in fact got the larger penance?

We can ask three questions of this new encyclical. 1. What is new in this encyclical? 2. What is missing or disappointing in this encyclical? 3. What in the encyclical calls for further development?

What is new in this encyclical?

Unquestionably, this encyclical, for the first time in Catholic social teaching, puts a positive emphasis on the market. The lack of any explicit treatment of the market as such has long been a strong *lacuna* in Catholic social teaching. Now, the Pope can say, straightforwardly, 'It would appear that, on the level of individual nations and of international relations, the free market is the most efficient instrument for utilizing resources and effectively responding to needs' (34).

Again, both the profit motive and the legitimacy of a limited self-interest are affirmed. 'The church acknowledges the legitimate role of profit as an indication that a business is functioning well. When a firm makes a profit, this means that productive factors have been properly employed and corresponding human needs have been duly satisfied' (35). About self-interest the Pope asserts: 'In fact, where self-interest is violently supp-ressed, it is replaced by a burdensome system of bureaucratic control which dries up the wellsprings of initiative and creativity' (25). Apologists for capitalism such as Michael Novak take comfort from such passages.

To be sure, every advantage yielded to the market and the profit-driven economy is quickly nuanced closely. Thus, the encyclical insists that there are new limits to the logic of the market. 'There are collective and qualitative needs which cannot be satisfied by market mechanisms. There are important human needs which escape its logic. There are goods which can not and must not be bought or sold' (39). It would have helped if the Pope had listed some of these goods. Do they include control over the mass media, the right to health care, access to electoral office?

This encyclical, for the first time in Catholic social teaching, presents specific criticisms of the operation of the bureaucracy in the social welfare state. Appealing to the principle of subsidiarity, it affirms: 'By intervening directly and depriving society of its responsibility, the social assistance state leads to a loss of human energies and an inordinate increase of public agencies, which are dominated more by bureaucratic ways of thinking than by concern for serving their clients, and which are accompanied by an enormous increase in spending. In fact, it would appear that needs are best understood and satisfied by people who are closest to them and who act as neighbours to those in need' (48).

What is missing in this encyclical?

I missed in this new social teaching a strong version of the recent Catholic insistence on justice as participation. To be sure, democracy and democratic forms come in for praise, as do 'the numerous efforts to which Christians made a notable contribution . . . in experimenting with various forms of participation in the life of the work place and in the life of society in general' (16). Yet, when dealing with trade unions, the encyclical sees them as vehicles for negotiating contracts and also valuable places where workers express themselves in their own culture of work (15). I missed the emphasis on worker co-determination and co-representation on industry boards one found in *Laborem Exercens*.

Finally, I fault a certain lack of a deeper social analysis in this encyclical. Thus, the Pope asserts: 'These criticisms are directed not so much against an economic system as against an ethical and cultural system. The economy in fact is only one aspect and one dimension of the whole of human activity. If economic life is absolutized, if the production and consumption of goods become the centre of social life and society's only value, not subject to any other value, the reason is to be found not so much in the economic system itself as in the fact that the entire socio-cultural system, by ignoring the ethical and religious dimension, has been weakened, and ends by limiting itself to the production of goods and services alone' (39). While this is true enough on the surface, it masks the ways in which the logic of the market has a built-in tendency toward market imperialism, a tendency to extend its logic where it does not belong. What Jürgen Habermas calls the 'colonization' of civil society by the logic of the market and the logic of the state is much more systemic than the encyclical suggests. Moreover, ethical and cultural systems never live as mere abstractions. They must be institutionalized. The privatization of ethics and religion when faced with the economy is not just a moral failure. It has systemic roots.

For further development

In the future, we will need to see a further development of the assertion: 'The individual today is often suffocated between two poles represented by the state and the marketplace. At times it seems as though he exists only as a producer and consumer of goods, or as an object of State administration. People lose sight of the fact that life in society has neither the market nor the state as its final purpose, since life itself has a unique value which the state and market must serve' (49). Surely, herein lies the germ for a worked-out Catholic theory of civil society which needs to be developed. Here, too, we see that both penitents deserve serious penances: socialism because it turns the logic of the state into a statist imperialism, capitalism because it does the same with market imperialism. And in the end the church's own contribution to social order will be judged, as this encyclical wisely notes, not just by its social *doctrine* 'but also by her concrete commitment and material assistance in the struggle against marginalization and suffering' (26).

John A. Coleman

I · God brings about Redemption through Cosmic and Historical Mediations

Human or 'Secular' History as a Medium for the History of Salvation or its Opposite: 'Outside the World there is No Salvation'

Johan de Tavernier

Does human, 'secular' history have a salvation-historical and eschatological dimension? According to Wolfhart Pannenberg, this question has never received sufficient attention in the past.[1] For believers, history is always related to a God whom we know as the ground and the dynamic of creation and salvation. *Extra mundum nulla salus*: outside the world there is no salvation. Ordinary, everyday history is the sphere of God's liberating action. For believers, it is meaningful to ask about the soteriological significance of everything that happens in human history. Does it bear a perspective of meaning or not? Is it saving or not? Believers cannot be content with a discussion of the political and social sphere which expresses only the political or social components. So theologians cannot be silent on non-theological problems. The principle that the theologian should not attempt to talk about other people's specialist concerns holds as a warning not to cripple the autonomy of the scientific interpretation of reality, but it does not mean that a theologian has nothing to say about this. More is at stake.

We can say something about this history of salvation or its opposite only on the basis of the interpretative experience of our history. But how shall we recognize anything as the history of salvation or its opposite – or, to put it another way, as being in keeping with the kingdom of God or in conflict with it? There is thus a question of theological legitimation (or non-legitimation). This is significant for the meaningfulness of the notion of the 'rule of God'. If talk about the kingdom of God is to continue to offer any basis, it is an abslolutely necessary task for Christians to examine developments which may or may not be saving and analyse them as salvation (or not) which is (or is not) in line with the kingdom of God. Talk about eschatological salvation loses any rational ground when there is no positive relationship between this claim to salvation and what is experienced by human beings as making them whole.[2] This is no easy task. There is a good deal of dissatisfaction about what some people feel to be improper theological legitimation or non-legitimation. However, a good deal of this resentment is to be explained by the way in which theologians sometimes work or have worked in the past. Some take too little account of a number of principles and criteria which must be followed.

I. Principles and criteria for a theological legitimation (or non-legitimation)

As for principles, I want first to point out the absolute need for theologians to be aware of the distinctive rationality and the laws of the problem area that they want to discuss. By way of illustration let us take the area of peace and war. If theology is to develop a good view of contemporary problems of peace, it will have to take fundamental account of war studies and peace studies. War studies are concerned empirically and analytically with the degree of large-scale conflicts, the amount that they cost, and how peace in one sense or another can be achieved within the field of tension of international relations. It is also interesting to know how those engaged in war studies describe the principles for the prevention or control of conflict, both in the long term and in the relatively short term. Thus theologians are primarily dependent on non-theological competence and prior knowledge, though they can also make their own critical contribution, above all in discussing the problem of peace in their own language field. Theological talk of peace begins where theologians raise theological and ethical questions about social developments, while at the same time being well aware of what rationality is being used.

The second principle is that it should be accepted that for believers, particular facts or particular political actions never have a neutral significance in relation to the kingdom of God in its aspect of the here and now. Their attitude is always either positive or negative: either it contributes towards salvation or it does not. Moreover Christians evaluate and appraise reality in a heightened way because their belief in God cannot and may not be a pretext for political or social neutrality. Christian faith implies an ethic which is directed towards a society that is good and worth living in. So theologians should take trouble to evaluate the facts on the basis of what is meaningful for human beings and what is not, what is salvation for human beings and what is not, in the perspective of God's promises. H. W. Vijver has called this process a theological process of decoding and legitimation.[3] It is a process by which an eschatological surplus or deficit is attached both to historical developments and to social and political actions. It should be noted that I am deliberately not speaking of a particular theological or political basis for an action but of a legitimation. The difference between legitimation and foundation can also be described like this: it is not possible for Christians to act politically in their own way or to provide the basis for a Christian politics. There is no third way, because it is impossible to work out a specifically Christian policy. However, a particular political project can be felt to be Christian. So the church does not get a normative role in solving problems of a political kind.[4]

Important questions arise here: what is the real nature of a theological decoding and legitimation, and what form does this process of legitimation take? I include both these questions under the heading of the criteria of a theological legitimation.

What criteria are necessary for recognizing something as being in line with salvation from God or regarding something as more or less in conflict with the will of God? Theologians can only legitimate something after the soundness of a particular political or social development has become sufficiently clear. However, investigation into whether or not something is sound is a typically ethical and hermeneutical concern, and not a matter for theology. In terms of method one has to maintain the distinction between a theological interpretation and an ethical interpretation which is arrived at with the help of other social sciences. Here we come up against a first difficulty: as such, the legitimate theological question whether 'in a particular event we must see a coming or an approaching or rather a rejection of the kingdom of God' is intrinsically a complex question because theology is dependent on other sciences in investigating whether or not this is the case. Before there can be any question of a theological mediation, a social-analytical and an ethical mediation is necessary. So judging whether or not something may rightly be recognized as salvation history is not a matter of a decision of faith, since it must be open to historical testing. We cannot investigate here the view of salvation history arising from a positivism of revelation.

It may sound strange, but Christians do not know better than others what can be regarded as salvation history and what cannot. It is not difficult to pass judgment on a dictatorship or a system of apartheid. But many other matters are more difficult. Does the actual behaviour and action of a pacifist or someone with a burdened conscience have the greatest claim to right action in terms of ethics, in other words to an action which may be recognized as action in keeping with the Kingdom of God? Or is the behaviour and the action of a non-pacifist ethically more correct, and does this lay claim to an eschatological surplus? It is not so easy to arrive at a good verdict here, even if we assume that all parties are prepared for a rational argument and inspired by good ethical motivation. Depending on the situation, this means that a limited plurality of possibilities and strategies for action may be noted as being conducive to wholeness and in line with God's kingdom of righteousness and love.

The following considerations are interesting here.

1. After ethical reflection, the more differentiated the opinions are about the value or otherwise of particular facts or strategies of action, the more hesitant one will be to call something salvation history in theological terms. I personally would make this depend on a dialogue within a church community. It there are fiercely opposed ethical opinions about particular facts, there will always be a tendency for individuals to present their own view as the only Christian one. Take, for example, the legitimation of a war by presenting it as a war willed by God or a just war. This clearly will not do. Such a claim obscures what at that moment is most necessary, namely a matter-of-fact ethical conversation. The more polarized the views on particular issues are, the more modest one must be in theological legitimation, and the more accurately one will have to use matter-of-fact argumentation or even matter-of-fact theological argumentation.[5] In general this will inevitably be the case when Christians are faced with the difficult task of opting for a particular political strategy. In my opinion, political ideologies are too ambivalent in theory and practice to be capable of theological legitimation.

2. Social and political salvation is always salvation to a lesser or greater degree; in other words, it is conducive to wholeness only to a limited extent. Of course the same thing can also be said about the opposite. Moreover, such salvation is extremely vulnerable and sometimes transitory. So we will never be able to speak of the coming of the kingdom of God, but only of *a* coming or approach of the kingdom of God or something that is in line with the kingdom of God.

3. Finally, I think that the most appropriate way of interpreting reality

theologically is through what can be called a negative procedure of legitimation. It seems to me easier for theology to indicate from its specific 'memory of the passion' how political practices and social developments which are not conducive to salvation are in conflict with the kingdom of God than to indicate what coincides with the will of God or may be identified as an approach of the kingdom of God. There is also something to be said for that theologically. However unsympathetic the concept of 'rule' may sound, we cannot avoid the fact that even for Jesus the experiential reality of 'God's rule' contains a judgment on history. Paul Ricoeur says that passing judgment on history in the light of the rule of God is the typical task of the prophet.[6] As is well known, Ricoeur introduces the prophet in a commentary on Merleau-Ponty's view of Koestler's claim that Marxism compels people to chose between an ethic of the yogi and an ethic of the commissar. The yogi strives through an inward change to achieve an uncompromising dispositional ethic, while the commissar seeks to change people through external pressure and is quite happy with the slogan 'the end justifies the means'. To avoid this exclusive choice between involvement and non-involvement, Ricoeur argues that a new figure is needed, namely the prophet, who according to Levinas embodies 'non-involvement' in involvement. The typical feature of prophets is that they formulate the transhistorical aspect in history, in this case the ethical demands in all their fullness, or what is humanly desirable (i.e. also what is wanted by God). Through his ethical protest, in which the simultaneity of detachment and involvement becomes clear (Levinas describes this as a 'difficult freedom'), the prophet maintains the tension in history.

The degree of difficulty in knowing theologically that anything is capable of improvement, in other words does not yet correspond to what God wills and thus to what is humanly desirable, is less than that of legitimating something in positive theological terms. In defining the degree of conflict with God's kingdom, however, the same difficulty emerges as in the positive procedure of legitimation. Here, too, an appeal to non-theological competence, in this case a social and ethical analysis, is really called for. It may sound somewhat strange, but it is the case that in the social sphere Christians do not know better than others what is sinful and what is not. The clearer the outcome of an analysis of reality in terms of social ethics, the more easily and more justifiably Christians may use the word 'sin'. Where there is unmistakable exploitation of people in the South by the North, doing 'institutionalized violence' to them, one can rightly use the description 'social sin'. However, that must be understood properly,

Talk about 'social sin' implies talk about social guilt. This talk differs from what Ricoeur calls subjective sinfulness or guilt (deliberate or intentional wrongs towards their parties).[7] Subjective sinfulness falls within the order of interpersonal forgiveness. Subjective guilt can be experienced after a searching of the conscience about the relationship between intention and actual action. Things are different in the case of social guilt, in which the accent comes to lie on the objective character of sinfulness. What we have here is an evil which no longer belongs in the order of forgiveness, because the significance of a particular action no longer coincides with my intention. According to Levinas, it is the social reality of the absent third party and the far-reaching socio-political structures which make it possible for me to be found guilty of something without having deliberately intended it.[8] In other words, social guilt is really objective guilt which is detached from a subjective awareness of guilt. A searching of the conscience or an analysis of my intentions is no longer meaningful here. One can only concede the injustice done and the accusations made and try as far as possible in action to avoid or remedy this social mistake. So social sin presupposes that responsibility goes further than the radius of action of the intention.

If we apply what has just been said to talk of 'social sin', then we can come to the conclusion that the greater the extent of negative experiences of contrast or the absence of salvation, if people can be made responsible for them, the more seriously and clearly we may speak of objective sinfulness.

II. The significance of a theological legitimation of the historical

So far we have been discussing a number of principles and criteria of a theological legitimation. Now the question arises how we express the soteriological significance of action and its value.

Social and political salvation is always salvation to a certain degree, and thus is relative and transitory. Nevertheless, this relative political and social salvation is also always qualified eschatologically. If we decode something as conducive to salvation, then we can also call it a 'first fruit' of eschatological salvation (Kuitert), a 'foretaste' of true salvation (Schillebeeckx), or an 'aperitif' before the definitive and perfect salvation from God (Alves).[9] This is not an analogous salvation, but it is certainly a foretaste of perfect salvation. The terms 'firstfruit', 'foretaste' and 'apertif' are also happy ones in that additionally they express the longing for perfect wholeness. Other authors express this in their own way. Thus Tillich speaks of 'fragmentary victories of the kingdom of God in history'. The consummation of the kingdom is the moment when God brings all the fragments together as a whole.[10] Pannenberg uses the idea of the 'anticipation of eschatological salvation' to indicate the saving character of events and actions.[11]

The terms 'firstfruits', 'foretaste', 'aperitif', 'fragment', 'anticipation' indicate that what we have is an appearance of the rule of God now and then, a coming or approach of the kingdom of God, and never its definitive coming. The eschatological proviso always remains in force. Nothing and no one can present itself as definite salvation. The kingdom of God can never be confused with a particular social programme. The necessary distance remains in force. Pannenberg aptly says, 'It remains future in the face of any present, even in the face of a future, better society'.[12] But the future character of the kingdom of God does not mean that this kingdom is an impotent 'otherworldliness'; rather, it is a dawning future. However, the proviso may not prevent us from associating saving moments with the kingdom of God, since it is unacceptable for Christians not to connect God's name with events conducive to salvation and perverse to associate it with whatever is not. Talk about saving events has no value if there is no basis for it in experience.

What is the value of giving an eschatological qualification to the historical? From experience we know that human action is partly determined by expectations which are cherished. In the same sense we can call the rule of God, which is growing but does not develop in a linear direction (as an eschatology in the process of realization), a well-founded expectation which can influence action. How do we see this influence? What does it mean that we see history as a mixture of salvation and its opposite?

According to F. Furger, the value of describing something as salvation from God or as in conflict with God's will (described in ethical terms) lies in the fact this approach takes up human history into a salvation-historical dynamic.[13] Expressing salvation history in history means that one is always alert to a concrete improvement in the *status quo*. In fact it is above all collective experiences of the absence of salvation or experiences of suffering which provoke the awareness of what is humanly desirable and which can be the stimulus to an action that can overcome suffering. What proves in this context to be humanly do-able can also be realized from a salvation-historical perspective. An action which is recognized as ethically good or ethically correct will be regarded by Christians as absolutely binding because of their specific involvement in the historical. At the same time it will be necessary to guard against what is humanly desirable functioning in a way that does not motivate people to achieve what is humanly do-able. On the other hand, one cannot stop at the short-sighted perspective of what is humanly do-able and in so doing lose sight of what is desirable. In this way the ethical action of Christians takes on a function which is qualified by the eschaton and therefore stimulating. This function is characterized by a striving for the greatest possible degree of humanity ('une justice toujours meilleure'), and through this also by a number of biblical ethical models which can play a significant role here. These include love of enemy and renunciation of retribution, a critical readiness to abandon one's own legal position, the discarding of short-sighted pre-judices, showing solidarity with others or having a watchful concern for the week, the disadvantaged and the defenceless who have no legal rights.

Finally, I also want to point out the implications of the salvation-historical interpretation of reality for ecclesiology. It is clear that the stimulation of a process for distinguishing between the history of salvation and its opposite is an important task for the church. Simply because history and salvation history run side by side, and salvation and liberation, disaster and evil, come about in this world and nowhere else, it follows that the church should have a much greater interest in what in fact happens in history. The church understands itself wrongly if it is too centred on itself and does not understand itself as being closely bound up with world history as it is experienced. Here Schillebeeckx's statement that 'the culture of the third that one has in common is always better than a controversy within the church' is fully valid.[14] The church can speak meaningfully about the rule of God only if it takes very seriously its practical hermeneutical task in connection with the expression of the dynamics of salvation history. The church community itself is also part of this dynamic. Therefore it is important for the church to be aware that its future is dependent on its qualitative presence in the future of the world and the fact that it expresses God's saving action in history or his judgment on it. Only if the church is successful here can it rightly regard itself as a credible sacrament of the salvation that God brings about in his world of creation.

III. The significance of the motif of future eschatology

Furthermore, the significance of the promise and the expectation of the kingdom of God means something more than the meaningfulness of the theological legitimation or delegitimation of the historical to which I have already referred. Salvation is not limited to historical salvation. Social salvation is not the only salvation that people may expect. The kingdom of God is not exhausted in present or future saving experiences. It is more than a progressive increase and extension of the dynamic of salvation history. It is an event here and now and hereafter.

There will always be a distance between the kingdom of God and the wholeness which is realized for human beings now and then. That means that for Christians there is no guarantee in history that history will turn out well. We cannot have any great certainty in our expectation of the good and the desirable, since the by no means negligible excess of suffering and evil in history remains. So as far as we are concerned there is no reason to expect that norm and fact will ever coincide.

Because of this break between a whole world which has already been attained and at the same time is still to be attained on the one hand and the kingdom of God on the other, God can remain God – that is, a reality which does not allow itself to be pinned down to our concepts of salvation. Precisely that gives human beings the freedom to be human, i.e. to define for themselves what passes for salvation or liberation and what does not.[15] Nevertheless, Christian salvation is at least 'earthly' salvation. It is to be found where the heart of history beats. In their true responsibility, all Christians share in the consummation of God's project of giving ultimate meaning to human life; in other words, in the all-embracing character of the process of liberation. But the consummation of the ultimate human future remains God's prerogative.

Human beings can realize the promise of their own being only as grace. Its basis and support lies in the fact that believers experience every small bit of salvation as a foretaste of the promise of the perfect salvation that God will give. The longing for liberation also ultimately takes on the connotation of being freed or redeemed from suffering and injustice. We do not know how and in what way this divine correction will come about, since no one can fathom the will of God. In order to give some expression to this positive indefinability, the New Testament uses three metaphors as symbols for human wholeness and health: (a) the kingdom of God as definitive salvation or the prevailing of a society of brothers and sisters in which there are no relationships that enslave; (b) the resurrection of the flesh or the perfect happiness of the individual, incarnated person; (c) the new heaven and the new earth, or the perfection of the 'ecological milieu' which human beings need.

What is the significance of this motif of future eschatology for historical action? As a utopian picture which is not without foundation for believers, these vivid visions of wholeness and perfection prevent us from seeing the existing historical order as an ideal order. Every social and economic order is capable of improvement. What is humanly desirable (justice, peace and the integrity of creation) draws attention to what is open to human criticism. From the difference between what is desirable and what can be criticized, in other words from the alienation between God and the world, there comes into being the critical force which prompts an ethical indignation of Christian inspiration and the call for liberation. To no small degree, this intensifies the character of liberation as a task and the longing for the definitive gift of liberation.

The relationship between liberation as a task and liberation as a gift of God is such as to have no significance for the epistemological question of what norms of action we should follow. The metahistorical kingdom does not offer any criterion for good action because this future reality does not have any precise content. The significance of the relationship lies at the level of motivation; the salvation which has already been attained is experienced in an interpretative way as a foretaste of the salvation promised by God. So the motivation lies in the way in which that which gives meaning rescues meaning. Of this A. Biesinger says that it has consequences for the activation, the intensity, the duration and the direction of human behaviour.[16]

From the horizon of meaning of the coming rule of God and the Kingdom of God, this means that the eschatological promise and its anticipation activates the will to act effectively and specifically, by indicating the discrepancy between the actual and the desirable which is sharpened up by the horizon of meaning. This horizon of meaning is a 'motive cause'; it is a stimulus to action. Secondly, it intensifies human action because it gives it a degree of urgency. Thirdly, this ethically inspired action never loses its significance within the Christian horizon of meaning. It remains permanently present, no matter what the circumstances, because it is always confirmed. So there can never be any question of resignation. Finally, the Christian motif also gives direction to action in so far as the Christian horizon of meaning implies a qualified idea of God and thus also a qualified commitment.

In this way the meaning of human action for the good is 'rescued'. It is given a basis with an absolute motivation. So we can also call the Christian horizon of meaning 'a system of values which carry conviction'. Whenever this motivation is integrated personally, the eschatological motif can become the 'soul' of the thought and action of Christians. The kingdom of God then becomes a principle of action through which they begin to look in a different way at what actually goes on in the world. A laid-back attitude to life does not fit in with the sense of living in a salvation-historical dynamic and in the expectation of the kingdom of God. 'Clad' in a well-founded hope Christians have a strongly existential trust in reality. The expectation of the kingdom of God not only keeps this hope alive but in addition is comfort, mercy and encouragement.

Conclusion

There are many things that, ethically speaking, Christians do not do better than non-Christians. But what they do, they do from a specific conviction and expectation. In this way the ethical takes on an eschatological dimension through which it is experienced as a collaboration with the grace of God.[17] So Christians are not indifferent to the historical. They have a sharpened evaluation of reality. However, support of good things and powerful opposition to things which run contrary to their eschatological expectation can never come about directly. The connection between salvation history and 'profane' human history always goes through a stage of ethical argument and theological hermeneutic which is furthered in dialogue (the theological-ethical qualification). So before arriving at a theological decoding and legitimation or delegitimation, Christians will always recognize that on purely human grounds, unemployment or apartheid really cannot be, since apartheid discriminates against people on the basis of the colour of their skin and their ancestry and unemployment is contrary to the right of everyone to work. Only at a secondary stage should Christians say that a society that allows these evils is not in accord with God's will, which is to be described in ethical terms (the eschatological qualification).

A third test as to whether or not salvation is at work is needed. One cannot continue to confess theoretically that God is a God of salvation without testing how, for example, statements of faith have a saving effect in practice. Because theology is concerned with reflection on the experience of (the coming of) salvation from God, it also has an obligation to itself to qualify history eschatologically, though not without first applying ethical qualifications.

Christians live in the tension between a transdescendent experience of grace, viz., the eschatology in Christ which has already been realized, and a transascendent experience of grace, viz., the future promise of salvation. The Christian expectation of the future is certainly a 'projected' expectation, but it is not just a projection, since there are good reasons for it. Through this tension, human and historical action is taken up in a dynamic

of salvation history which places two stresses. On the one hand unpreced-
ented importance is attached to the 'must': what is offered as a possibility
of humanization must be realized effectively. On the other hand the
possibility of ethical action so frees and liberates from the compulsion of
the 'must' that it is also in a position to do what must be done. It is no
coincidence that J. Gustafson points out that in the statement 'ought
implies can', by the introduction of the eschatological motif into the
ethical, attention can primarily be paid to the 'can'.[18] God puts us in a
position to fulfil our ethical duty.

Translated by John Bowden

Notes

1. W. Pannenberg, 'Can Christianity do without an Eschatology?', in G. B. Caird,
W. Pannenberg, I. T. Ramsey et al., *The Christian Hope*, Theological Collections 13,
London 1970, 25ff.
2. E. Schillebeeckx, *Church. The Human Story of God*, London and New York
1990, 30–3.
3. The terms 'decode' and 'legitimate' are taken over from H. W. Vijver, *Theologie
en bevrijding. Een onderzoek naar de relatie tussen eschatologie en ethiek in de
theologie van G. Gutiérrez, J. C. Scannone en R. Alves*, Amsterdam 1985, 167.
4. H. W. Vijver, 'Uitdagingen voor de theologie in Latijns Amerika', in
K. U. Gabler, G. Manenschijn et al., *Geloof dat te denken geeft. Opstallen aangeboden
aan Prof. dr. H. M. Kuitert*, Baarn 1989, 286.
5. G. Manenschijn, *Eigenbelang en christelijke ethiek. Rechtvaardigheid in een door
belangen bepaalde samenleving*, Baarn 1982, 145.
6. P. Ricoeur, 'Le Yogi, le Commissaire, le Prolétaire et le Prophète. À propos de
"Humanisme et terreur" de Maurice Merleau-Ponty', in *Christianisme social* 57, 1949,
41–54.
7. Cf. id., *La Symbolique du Mal*, Paris 1960.
8. Cf. E. Levinas, 'Le Moi et la Totalité', in *Revue de Métaphysique et de Morale* 59,
1974, 353–73. For a discussion see R. Burggraeve, *From Self-Development to
Solidarity. An Ethical Reading of Human Desire in its Socio-Political Relevance
according to Emmanuel Levinas*, Louvain 1985, 101f.
9. H. Kuitert, 'Hoe messiaans kan politiek zijn?' in *Gereformeerd Weekblad*, 1982,
236–43; E. Schillebeeckx, *Christ*, London and New York 1980, 746; R. Alves, *A
Theology of Human Hope*, New York 1969, ²1971, 119–31, 151, 155.
10. P. Tillich, *Systematic Theology*, Vol. 3, Chicago 1963, reissued London 1975,
394.
11. W. Pannenberg, 'Das Problem einer Begründung der Ethik und die
Gottesherrschaft', in id., *Theologie und Reich Gottes*, Gütersloh 1971, 75.
12. Ibid., 73.
13. F. Furger, 'Sozialethik in heilsgeschichtlicher Dynamik', in H. Rotter (ed.),

Heilsgeschichte und ethische Normen, Quaestiones Disputatae 99, Freiburg, Basle and Vienna 1984, 128f.

14. E. Schillebeeckx, 'Spreken over God in een context van bevrijding', in *Tijdschrift voor Geestelijk Leven* 40, 1984, 23.

15. H.Kuitert, 'De vrede van God en de vrede van de wereld', in A. van den Beld and E. Schroten (eds.), *Kerk en vrede*, Baarn 1976, 73.

16. A. Biesinger, 'Der christliche Sinnhorizont als Motivation für ethisches Handeln?', in H. Weber and D. Mieth (eds.), *Anspruch der Wirklichkeit und christlicher Glaube. Probleme und Wege theologischer Ethik heute*, Düsseldorf 1980, 285.

17. D. Mieth, 'Quellen und normierende Instanzen in der christlichen Ethik', in J. Blank and G. Hasenhüttel (eds.), *Erfahrung, Glaube und Moral*, Düsseldorf 1982, 46.

18. J. Gustafson, *Theology and Christian Ethics*, Philadelphia 1974, 55f.

II · 'Justice, Peace and the Integrity of Creation'

A. 'The Conciliar Process'

The Ecumenical Dynamic of 'Justice, Peace and the Safeguarding of Creation'

René Coste

By the very title of this article I am immediately taking sides. While enthusiastically welcoming the invitation addressed to the churches by the Sixth Assembly of the World Council of Churches to a 'mutual commitment (covenant) to justice, peace and the integrity of all creation', I am not adopting the description which it gave of the 'conciliar process'. For as Catholics (and Orthodox) conceive it, a council is a gathering of bishops. Certainly we must hope that one day the various churches can meet in a real council. We must pray fervently to the Holy Spirit – 'the master of the impossible' – and open all our hearts in this direction. But this blessed day has not yet arrived.

What I shall not be accepting, either, is the expression 'ecumenical process' which is current in Catholic circles. I shall talk of an 'ecumenical dynamic' in order to indicate my conviction that the invitation of the World Council of Churches has started a movement of broad ecumenical dialogue and cooperation which must not cease to deepen and develop for the greater good of the churches and humankind.

According to the usage which has now prevailed in the French-speaking world, I shall not retain the literal translation of the third term of the trilogy ('integrity of creation'), although English usage keeps it as it is. In conformity to the official French translation of the documents, I shall speak of the 'safeguarding of creation' (the Germans have chosen an identical option). In my view it would be better to talk of the 'management' of creation, in order better to bring out the profound significance of the basic biblical texts.[1] This expression in fact has two advantages: on the one hand it marks the limits of human power since human beings are only managers (responsible before God the Creator and their human brothers and sisters), and on the other it leaves vast scope to human freedom and creativity, since the manager is always allowed considerable initiative. Thinking in particular of the Gospel parables, one could also talk of the stewardship of creation, as is done in certain English-speaking theological circles.

The point of view that I shall express in the present article will be at the same time that of a historian, of a theologian and one who is involved in the dynamic (since I was one of the members of the international preparatory committees for the ecumenical meetings in Basle and Seoul. In Basle I was part of the group which prepared the 'Final Document', and at Seoul I was a member of the delegation from the Holy See. I am also a member of the new European ecumenical working party.)

I. 'Peace and Justice for the Whole of Creation' (The European Ecumenical Assembly at Basle, 15–22 May 1989)

Various national, regional and world meetings on the questions of JPSC (the abbreviation I shall adopt) have stressed not only the global dimension of the dynamic but also its diversity. As far as I know, the national meetings which took place in West and East Germany (Erfurt, Stuttgart, Dresden, etc. in 1988/89) produced the most important texts. Among the great regional gatherings I would mention the conferences or meetings organized in the Pacific region (September 1988), in Europe (May 1989), and in Latin America (December 1989). There have also been a number of regional meetings for women. The theological perspectives of many meetings with a confessional character have greatly enriched the JPSC dynamic: the Orthodox approach (Sofia 1987 and Minsk 1989), the Roman Catholic approach (the Pontifical Council on 'Justice and Peace', Vatican 1989) and the reflections of the World Reformed Alliance (Seoul 1989). Because of the limits of space, here I shall have to content myself with a brief account of the most important regional meeting, the European Ecumenical Assembly in Basle (15–21 May 1989), which took as its slogan 'Peace and Justice for the Whole of Creation', and the World Assembly at Seoul.

It was in September 1986 that the Ninth General Assembly of the Conference of European Churches (KEK) decided to arrange a JPSC European Ecumenical Assembly and to invite the Council of European Conferences of Bishops (CCEE) to participate. After ten months of reflection the Seventeenth General Assembly of the CCEE decided at the end of August 1987 to accept the invitation of the KEK. The secretariats were established in September 1987, and the preparatory group, jointly nominated by the KEK and the CCEE, met in full in December of the same year. It was decided that the assembly would bear the title 'Peace and Justice'. It brought together 700 delegates (approximately half KEK and half CCEE), nominated by the churches and the organizers. It was to be held in Basle in Pentecost week 1989 (a choice motivated by the major financial contributions offered by the city and the canton, the city's very rich religious history, and its geographical situation, at the crossroads of three countries and of the French-speaking and German-speaking cultures). It was to be a gathering for prayer, dialogue and common reflection and for sisterly and brotherly sharing. Alongside the official gathering, the participation of others was encouraged, specifically of the local population and the ecumenical associations which had created 'a European network to further justice, peace and the safeguarding of creation', and of the groups which had gathered under the name 'Workshop for the Future of Europe'. The gigantic and complex organization functioned admirably, thanks to the enthusiasm and devotion of the organizers and their collaborators at all levels.[2]

I would like first of all to stress the place of prayer at the meeting. The organizers had wanted it to have first place, both because the basic approach was that of the faith of the representatives of the European churches and because they thought that it was in the prayer meetings that the participation of the largest possible number of Christians, which was keenly sought after, could best be realized. Their wishes were fulfilled beyond their wildest hopes. The opening celebration and the morning celebrations in the Protestant cathedral, and the closing celebration in the square in front of the cathedral, were great moments of ecumenical liturgy and shared fervour. I think that this remarkable success was largely due to the work and the happy initiatives of the sub-committee of the preparatory group responsible for organizing the prayer meetings. As Mgr Nicolas Wyrwel remarked, a number of delegates and visitors found the offices of prayer at Basle even more significant than the declarations of the 'Final Document'. He added that for everyone 'the equal participation of women in worship had been a notable sign, above all in fact because this participation seemed to be a spontaneous one'.

On the whole, the lectures and the discussions formed a contribution of high quality to the shared reflections. Those who gave them and the titles of their contributions were as follows: the Orthodox Archbishop Cyril of Smolensk on 'The Ecology of the Spirit'; the Right Hon. David Steel, a British Member of Parliament, on 'Reconciliation in Europe, Heritage and Vision': Cardinal Etchegaray on 'The Responsibility of Christians in a Time of Crisis'; Mrs Aruna Gandasong from India on 'The South calls us to a New Order'; Mrs M. L. de Pintasilgo from Portugal on 'Justice'; Mario Pavan from Italy on 'The Environment. A Role for Christians in World Ecology: Safeguarding Creation'; and Mrs A. M. Schoenherr from West Germany on 'Peace'. Nor should the speeches by two young women, Miss Sylvia Raulo from Finland and Miss Isabella Nepoli from Italy, be forgotten. One could have listened to Professor C. F. von Weizsäcker for a long time; he was undoubtedly one of the great promoters of the JPSC dynamic.[3]

The working parties (twenty in number) were intended to encourage the active participation of all the delegates in communal reflection. The 'hearings' – though outside the official assembly – also made a contribution here: these were lectures and discussions, thirty-three in number, which occupied the evenings between 16 and 19 May and in all brought together more than 20,000 people. (They were organized by twenty-seven institutions and movements grouped in a 'network'.) There were also the activities of the 'Workshop for the Future of Europe' (which brought together 118 groups from 14 European countries).

The young people undoubtedly contributed towards the open and friendly climate of the days in Basle, which was characterized by a readiness for commitment and a truly ecumenical spirit. They regretted that they did not have more representatives among the official delegates. Unfortunately a bad mistake was made in providing accommodation for some of them (the stewards) in Civil Defence shelters (i.e. installations planned to provide protection in time of war). Many of them were shocked by this. It proved possible to relocate them among families. The members of the Conference of European Churches made apologies to the young people concerned.

The organizers had planned that the meeting should produce a brief 'Message' and a substantial 'Final Document'. Normally, the preparation of the first text should have been easy, and that proved to be the case. It was adopted almost unanimously (of 502 voters, 489 were for, 3 against, and there were 10 abstentions). The production of the 'Final Document' extended over several months (two successive plans had been sent to the delegates before the conference), and was the object of intensive work during the assembly itself, right up to the last moment. Thanks to the remarkable spirit of ecumenical dialogue and the concern to listen to one another which marked the work of the editorial group and the assembly, the result was spectacular: a close-packed and long document (33 single-spaced typescript pages in the French-language edition) on very complex social problems. It was adopted by almost all the delegates at the assembly (95.4%).

The six chapters of the document were rigorously interconnected. Chapter 1 indicated in what capacity and what spirit the signatories were making their statement: they were speaking as delegates of the churches of Europe, listening to 'what the Holy Spirit is saying to the churches today', about the God of life who 'tells us to renounce injustice, violence and exploitation' and calls us to conversion (no. 1).

Chapter 2 was about the challenges to be met in the three spheres of justice, peace and the environment. Rightly, there was stress on their interdependence, which was illustrated by the cases of the Amazon rain forest and the Horn of Africa. Reference was made to the problems of demographic growth, the oppression of women and the violation of their rights (through sexism and the feminization of poverty) and to technology. It was made clear that the 'abusive utilization' of technology was 'responsible for the growing exploitation of the environment which, unless it is restrained, will lead to its degradation' (no. 18).

Chapter 3 (The 'Faith that we Affirm') is basic to the spirit of those who produced the document: the whole thrust of the later chapters depends on it. It forcibly affirms several essential points of the Christian faith which are shared by all. First of all comes faith in the Creator God, the trinitarian God, 'who in his mercy is revealed to humanity in Jesus Christ' (no. 21). It would be wrong to accuse this chapter of not being sufficiently christo-logical. While it is true that there was a concern to give preference to the trinitarian approach, christology was certainly not forgotten. The basic Christian anthropology which is expressed in nos. 22 and 23 is formulated in the tradition of Orthodox theology, following an amendment (which was lightly revised) produced by a group of Orthodox Christians. Then the three themes of the 'gospel of peace', of hope and of the church as the people of God and the body of Christ in the power of the Holy Spirit, are touched on. I would draw attention to the remarkable synthetic formulation of the doctrine of non-violence in accordance with the gospel that can be found at no. 32. It occurs in the wake of a very welcome reassessment which is being made in the contemporary church, in which the right to 'legitimate (or just) defence' is still maintained. Apart from a very tiny minority of Christians, one could say that there is a real ecumenical consensus here. I personally would not hesitate to recognize non-violence as a command of the gospel, but would point out that this commandment, like the whole of the gospel ethic, is subject to the supreme regulation of the commandment of love.

Chapter 4 (Confession of Sin and Conversion to God, Metanoia) proposes a penitential approach. Chapter 5 ('Towards Tomorrow's Europe') takes up the expression 'our common European home' which was popularized by Gorbachev. Some people feared that it indicated a bias in favour of the Soviet leader and that there was a degree of ambiguity about it. The editorial group spent a long time reflecting on this problem. Finally, it concluded that the expression was not Gorbachev's property and that it was quite possible to suggest a conception independent of his: besides, as the phrase was an evocative one, it was worth keeping. In my view the use made of it in the document is hard to quarrel with. it necessarily calls to mind the 'planetary village' dear to Toynbee.

The long and important Chapter VI (Basic Affirmations, Commitments, Recommendations and Future Perspectives) in fact begins with affirmations and commitments. Then it proposes detailed recommendations: first of all on the JPSC trilogy, then on dialogue with the inhabitants of other regions of the world, and finally on the continuation of the ecumenical process in Europe.

I shall remember the statement that 'it is essential that the basic concern for justice, peace and the safeguarding of creation should not be dissociated from the mission of the church to proclaim the gospel' (no. 79). One could even have wished for a statement which said forthrightly that the promotion of peace, justice and the safeguarding of creation is an integral dimension of the mission of evangelization which falls to the church. *Stress on the social dimension of evangelization is one of the great new features of theology and pastoral work in our time*. The position taken on this question by the Basle Document shows a real ecumenical consensus. It is vital to stress this new dimension of evangelization, since on the one hand it is a demand of the word of God, which for too long Christians have failed to recognize, and on the other hand it is still far from being sufficiently recognized – or in certain theological and pastoral spheres it is distorted.

How does one evaluate the assembly that I have just described? On the whole, reactions to it have been very positive. The eminent historian Fr Carlo Maria Martini did not hesitate to write that it was a historical and pentecostal event, that it was characterized by a strong ethical commitment, and that it was a positive example of convergence.[4] My view is that it was a 'significant assembly of the people of God', since in one way or another the Christians who took part in it represented the whole of Europe (with the exception of Albania, still imprisoned under a dictatorial and totalitarian régime). I have shown that to a high degree it was a gathering characterized by prayer, sisterly and brotherly sharing, and reflection in the light of faith. One cannot but regard the 'Final Document' as the imperfect but real concrete expression of a great effort at ecumenical reflection, which calls on all the churches of Europe to face the great social problems on their continent clearly and courageously.

II. The World Assembly on Justice, Peace and the Safeguarding of Creation (Seoul, 5–12 March 1990)

The group responsible for preparing the JPSC world assembly was formed in 1988, with the participation of the Roman Catholic church. However, the church reserved the freedom to decide whether or not it should join those invited to the assembly. It was decided that the assembly should take place in Seoul from 5–12 March 1990. In organizing the whole event, the group spent considerable time producing a working document, which was the subject of two successive drafts sent to the churches and the delegates. The second draft had the very expressive title *Between the Flood and the Rainbow*, with the subtitle, *Making a Covenant for Justice, Peace and the Safeguarding of Creation*. The first and longest part (31 typescript pages in the French-language edition) was about 'the realities with which we are confronted' (Section A) and 'the confession of the covenant community' (Section 8). The second part (7 pages) contained the text of eight 'Affirmations', and the third part (9 pages) suggested three 'acts of covenant'. It proved that a number of delegates did not receive this second text in time.

Almost a thousand people (791 participants and 267 journalists) met in Seoul in the weight-lifting pavilion of the Olympic park for the first large meeting of the world assembly, on the evening of 5 March. Among the 404 delegates with voting rights, 36% were women and 64% men; less than 10% were young people. By continents, the 404 delegates were divided as follows: Africa 17%, Latin America 8%, North America 19%, Asia 18%, the Caribbean 4%, Europe 30%, the Middle East 1% and the Pacific 3%.

The 79 participants were divided into 404 delegates, 60 advisers, 114 visitors, 34 stewards, 118 staff and 22 members of the local committee. Of this total, 105 were Catholics. The budget for the assembly was raised to a million Swiss francs. Despite its limited involvement, the Holy See contributed a tenth of this budget.

The vast area which had been put at our disposal was ill suited to a meeting of prayer and work like ours. But we were at ease there. Except on the Sunday (when everyone took part in worship in one of the churches or chapels in Seoul, depending on their confessional allegiance), the day began with a substantial time of prayer into which were inserted testimonies or homilies. There followed plenary assemblies or working parties.

Unlike those who organized the Basle assembly, who had wanted a range of substantive lectures, the Seoul organizers opted for homilies and testimonies. The only major address planned had been entrusted to Frank Chikane, Secretary General of the Churches of South Africa (SACC). He was lively and made a strong appeal to the emotions of those involved. The four testimonies on 7 March were particularly striking: the first, by Anne Pattel-Gray, was on the drama of the aborigines and the islanders in Australia, who had been stripped of their land; the second was by Zonra Azirou, an Algerian woman who arrived in France at the age of six and suffered a severe shock from anti-North African racism; the third, by Nasko Iyori, was on the drama of the Philippine women doomed to prostitution because of the extreme poverty of their families, whom they wanted to help to survive; the fourth was by Felix Sugirtharaj, on the inhumanity of the condition of the 200 million 'untouchables' in India. The forum of 7 March was addressed by the theologian Jorge Peixote, from Uruguay, by Carl Friedrich von Weizsäcker and by the Governor of Ohio, Richard Celeste, on threats to life. The same day, the sermon by the American woman bishop Barbara Harris caused an incident. To show their disapproval that she had been allowed to speak in an act of worship, the Orthodox had left the room. I can do no more than mention the other speakers: Bishop Simon Sungsoo Kim, Cardinal Kim, Marga Bührig, Emilio Castro . . . All the speeches were of real interest as testimonies or expressions of convictions. However, all in all they did not help much in deepening the analysis of social realities or theological reflection, and this was to prove the great weakness of the assembly.

I mentioned above the second draft of the working paper. The organizers had decided that the first part would be studied by the assembly and freely commented on by all, but that it would remain as it was. It might possibly be 'received' or 'rejected', but it would not be rewritten. So it would remain a simple working paper. There is no doubt that the assembly felt frustrated by such a procedure. It had the impression that the document was escaping it. Besides, many people – at least in the working parties or in private conversations – formulated serious objections at a theological level about its analysis of human realities. The plenary assembly clearly revealed this marked dissatisfaction on the part of a large number of its members. The criticism from the representatives of the Orthodox churches was the most incisive, though the document which they produced (four typescript pages), signed by two metropolitans, was not made public on this occasion. The result was that the offending text was abandoned. It was simply a completely outdated step in communal reflection.

As the two other parts of the working paper were wholly within the competence of the assembly, reactions towards them were more favourable, even if they were substantially revised. The 'Affirmations' were increased to ten: the need to give account to God of all exercise of power (I); the divine option in favour of the poor (II); the equal value of all races and all peoples (III); men and women are created in the image of God (IV); truth is the foundation of a community of free beings (V); the peace of Jesus Christ (VI); all creatures are loved by God (VII); the earth is the Lord's (VIII); the dignity and commitment of the younger generation (IX); human rights are given by God (X). The explanation given was evocative (a document of eleven typescript pages).

The act of covenant adopted by the assembly contained four commitments:

I. To an equitable local, national, regional and international economic order, from which all could benefit; to freedom from the slavery of all external debt.

II. To the real security of all peoples and nations; to the demilitarization of international relations; against militarism and doctrines and systems of natural security; to a culture of non-violence as a force for change and liberation.

III. To the establishment of a culture which respects creation; to the preservation of the gift of the terrestrial atmosphere so as to feed and maintain life on earth; to fight the causes of atmospheric changes which threaten to change the climate of the earth and bring great suffering everywhere in the world.

IV. To eliminate racism and discrimination against all human beings; to the destruction of the walls which divide human beings because of their ethnic origin; to the elimination of forms of economic, political and social behaviour which perpetuate the sin of racism or allow individuals to perpetuate it.

The document ran to twelve typescript pages. Only the introduction and the essential terms of the commitments were adopted by the assembly, which did not have time to pronounce on the propositions which spelt them out, some of which would have needed major redrafting.

We know that the Holy See, having for a while envisaged a more committed participation (which would have been an innovation in its relationships with the assemblies organized by the World Council of Churches), finally decided in principle on a more limited presence (with an official delegation of twenty 'consultants', which the assembly put in the category of 'advisers'). It is also clear that this decision caused great disappointment, not only to the ecumenical authorities but also within the Catholic church itself. Many people saw this as a sign of ecumenical disengagement (some did not hesitate to lay this at the door of John-Paul II himself) or a lack of interest in the most burning problems of contemporary society.

How can one fail to be surprised at the second interpretation when one knows the social teaching of the contemporary papacy (for example in the encyclical *Sollicitudo rei socialis*, which is so valued in ecumenical circles)? Nor does the hypothesis of ecumenical disengagement stand serious examination.

The Catholic church is certainly not uninterested in the ecumenical dynamic of JPSC. What the Holy See does want is for it always to be conducted in an authentic ecclesial approach (in conformity with the mission entrusted by Christ to his church), based on a valid theology and a serious objective analysis of the realities of life in society. That is certainly a demanding attitude. But is it not beneficial in the long term for the ecumenical movement itself? Even at Seoul, many people who spoke with me (Reformed and Lutherans as well as Orthodox) did not mince their words in acknowledging this. So Mgr Basil Meeking, head of the delegation from the Holy See, was able to give public expression to the profound interest of the Catholic church in the Seoul assembly and the whole dynamic in which it was a historic step. His statement was warmly received by the whole assembly.

For those who had had the splendid ecumenical experience of Basle, Seoul could not but bring some disappointment. Some found it very sad. Personally, being familiar with the preparations, I expected this. But in conversations we were agreed that we should not be content with a simple comparison. The difficulties which had to be surmounted at a world level

(Seoul) were inevitably greater than those at a European level (Basle). The legitimate disappointment should not make us judge unfairly what we experienced during that memorable week in March 1990.

What can be said from a positive point of view? First, that it was worth having Christians from all over the world together to pray, to share their faith in the word of God, to reflect together on the most serious problems of society in our time (the JPSC trilogy includes almost all of them) and to encourage one another to tackle them in the light of the gospel. And despite the cultural and ideological divergences, the atmosphere was sisterly and brotherly, and the Christian faith was the common denominator. Despite all the imperfections, this was a world 'first' that we experienced together. Most of the testimonies that we heard were forceful. They drew attention to the terrible injustices and the frightful suffering that countless million human beings (our brothers and sisters) have to cope with. Even if the analyses implicit in the whole process were summary – and even open to question – the facts that they denounced were no less real. It is important to realize the real affliction which they represent, and we must strive courageously to bring them to an end – as soon as possible.

Negatively, it has to be said first of all that the theology of the first part of the working paper was open to discussion (this seems to have been the view of all the really competent theologians). In particular, it smacked more of the Old Testament than the New. Furthermore, it often lacked a substantial and sure analysis of the realities studied (one cannot be content with testimonies, however sincere). Moreover, there was not sufficient distinction between the specific mission of the churches towards society (Seoul did not have to be a second United Nations!) and the approach of a political assembly or a cultural club. And the criticism of ideologies was far from satisfactory.

In particular, I share the position of the Orthodox participants over the concept of covenant: 'We believe that the covenant of God with humankind, which has been established in the body and blood of Jesus Christ, our saviour and redeemer . . . cannot be broken and that it is eternal. That is why we reject any possibility that human beings can break, and thus renew and re-establish, the covenant with God.'

In spite of that, after weighing the pros and cons, I think that all in all the Seoul assembly was a positive event, even though one could have wished for more (and that would have been possible had the preparatory group – which met in a very friendly atmosphere – been as concerned with reciprocal ecumenical listening as had been the preparatory group for the Basle assembly). It was my duty as a theologian to express criticisms as I see them. But I think that what we experienced at Seoul can represent a step forward, if one can make the adjustments that are needed.

Since then, the Central Committee of the World Council of Churches has decided that the Council should reaffirm its long-term commitment to the JPSC dynamic. In particular it has stated: 'It will be necessary to move towards structural modifications in the work under way and to find appropriate resources for offering the churches and movements a centre for exchanges and stimulating information.' As far as Europe is concerned, a new international working party has been formed which will present proposals to the relevant authorities in the KEK and the CCEE.

Despite the difficulties encountered in Seoul, it is important for Christians throughout the world to unite in promoting justice, peace and the safeguarding of creation with ardour, in the light of the Word of God. What matters is to pursue this course with perseverance, learning lessons from its defects and hoping that the improvements needed can be made.

The basic problem lies in the sphere of methodology. We need a theology with a sufficiently sound base which can also prove acceptable to all the great Christian traditions (the experience at Basle showed that this was possible). We also need an objective analysis of realities which can be accepted as valid by well-informed observers. We also need agreements on the relationship that needs to be established between the social sciences, the ideologies, ethics, theology and the commitments of the churches and of individual Christians. How do we link these commitments to the Word of God which, while providing us with essential illumination, directs us towards our responsibility? And what is the specific mission of the churches towards life in society? Furthermore, a church assembly (and an ecumenical assembly) must not be a political assembly, even if it aims to make a political impact.

In this perspective, it seems to me desirable above all to organize a world ecumenical discussion of a scientific kind which would try to take account of the most serious problems in basic methodology (basing itself, moreover, on earlier research by the churches and the World Council of Churches). The preparation of this would need to be fully ecumenical, since the choice of themes and speakers would be crucial.

It is important for the Christian communities throughout the world to awaken to the JPSC dynamic. If it is only the affair of a thin layer of senior officials, then it will not fulfil its necessary mission. National and regional assemblies seem eminently desirable, provided that they work by the method that I have recommended. Then one could envisage a new world assembly (in seven years?), prepared by a truly representative international committee. Problems keep cropping up again. But a 'peace council' would only be a stage. The important thing is to have a permanent ecumenical JPSC dynamic on a much broader scale.

Translated by John Bowden

Notes

1. Cf. my book *Paix, justice, gérance de la création*, Paris 1989.
2. Cf. my article 'Paix et justice pour la création entière. Le Rassemblement oecuménique européen de Bâle (15–21 mai 1989)', in *Documente-Episcopat*, published by the French conference of bishops, January 1990. See also *Rassemblement oecuménique européen de Bâle, Paix et Justice pour la création entière*, the French edition of the official texts and documents, Paris 1989.
3. C. F. von Weizsäcker, *Die Zeit drängt*, Munich and Vienna 1987.
4. *La civiltà Cattolica*, 16 September 1989, 462–71.

Conciliar Process: The Analysis of a Term

Anton van Harskamp

The conciliar process is meant to mobilize people in the churches. It began with the call to all the churches from the General Assembly of the World Council of Churches in Vancouver in 1983. It was an appeal to come together at all levels of the churches to take part in the struggle against the world-wide threats to life. This happened out of a sense that humanity was moving in a negative direction, into a completely new situation. It is the situation which has arisen through the possibility that human beings may do the greatest injustice, i.e. annihilate life on earth. And precisely this situation of a humankind which is approaching the apotheosis of self-destruction and anticipates this every day in the suffering of the poor makes a new form of conciliar co-operation necessary. So it was thought that the situation was one in which a council was necessary. For the God of life seems to be being pushed out by human systems which are divinizing themselves. The call consisted in the urgent question whether commitment to peace, justice and the integrity of creation can be built up from below through a solidarity in prayer, discussion and decision. By doing this, the churches in the ecumenical movement wanted to indicate that they in their turn had heard the call going out from those whose life was directly threatened.

In the meantime it has become unclear whether the term 'conciliar process' is still going to be used on a large scale in the ecumenical movement. At the provisional climax of 'the process', the international gathering which was held in Seoul in March 1990, the term had to be abandoned, for theological reasons. So we may expect that while the term will not disappear immediately – since it has become familiar in a number of churches – in the long run it will not be retained.

In this survey I want first to reflect on the plausibility of the objections to the term and then on the disadvantages of its disappearance. Finally I shall offer some suggestions about the theological work that needs to be done if the churches really want to honour the intention of the conciliar process. The question here is whether the action of the churches demonstrates that they are really listening to the cry for just conditions which resounds from creation.

I. Tensions in the concept

The term 'conciliar process' did not just appear within the ecumenical movement in 1983. It is directly related to the concept of 'conciliarity'. And that concept is the result of an assimilation of thought about the significance of councils for the life of the church. So if the term 'conciliar process' is to be understood properly, it is necessary to indicate a few historical points which serve as landmarks in this development. After that we shall look at the theological term 'conciliarity'.

First of all we need to know that from the beginning, i.e. from the 1960s, concern for councils and for conciliar forms was primarily set in the hermeneutical perspective of the question of unity between the churches. And this question was in the first instance regarded as a question which primarily called for a theological and dogmatic solution. Certainly the ecumenical movement grew out of a Christian peace movement; and particularly in the 1960s, the world divided by violence and racism provided a stimulus to new dogmatic and theological reflection on the unity of the church. However, certainly up to the beginning of the 1970s, attention to all concepts connected with the word 'council' remained within the ideal context of a dogmatic and theological argument about the nature of the church. Whether people wanted it or not, as a result an obligation remained to the old idea that the dogmatic and theological content of the unity of the church provided the foundation and gave the direction for the ethics and action of the church. We shall see that this hermeneutical perspective on the specifically theological nature of the church produces considerable tension, specifically in relation to the concept of 'conciliarity'.

The New Delhi Assembly of 1961 identified the nature of the church unity that was sought as 'one fully committed fellowship'. This exists at each particular place where the church is and at the same time embraces all places. Above all stimulated by the announcement and the course of the Second Vatican Council, people then began to study the question how visible forms of conciliar discussion in the early church contributed to the formation of the unity of the early church. They began to ask what theological conditions led to the emergence of the church at councils as one church with authority both outwardly and inwardly. The questions which were initially in the background here were: Could the World Council itself be a platform for organizing a council? Is one of the main aims of the quest for Christian ecumenism an authentically universal council?

Next, at a Faith and Order Conference in England, at Bristol in 1967, a report was discussed which spoke of 'the conciliar process' (!) in the early church. Looking back on the reactions to this report, one cannot escape the feeling that there was already a degree of amibiguity here. For on the one hand the report indicated that the present situation of the church is not comparable with the early church, because at that time there was a real fellowship, whereas now there is a confrontation between a multiplicity of church communities. But on the other hand the report argued that conciliarity is of the essence of the church – and thus is clearly of the essence of all existing Christian churches. So the conciliar process should go on within the separated churches. And on the basis of this last assumption it was optimistically concluded that the World Council could be a tool in preparing for a universal council. This last thought was then later taken up by the Uppsala assembly by way of an invitation to further discussion. At an interesting Faith and Order conference in Louvain in 1971 the mood had become rather more pessimistic. This marked the provisional end of thinking about councils and conciliarity. Here in fact the idea of a council to be held one day and prepared for by the churches was markedly relativized. And a distinction was drawn between the council as an event which might possibly express the unity of Christianity in an unknown future and conciliarity as an essential structure in the life of the church.

If we are to get a view of the present 'conciliar process', we need to look more attentively at the concept of conciliarity which was developed at that time. It is an extremely complex concept. Often it is used only as a description of the fact that down the centuries Christians have come together at all levels within the church. But that is not its deepest significance. The concept – which we must not confuse with the historical conciliar movement, with its orientation above all on canon law – must be distinguished from the term 'conciliar fellowship'. For the latter term relates to a practicable model for a relationship between church communi-ties, whereas 'conciliarity' is primarily a theological and normative term which in a manner of speaking denotes the transcendental depth of being the church. It is an existential of being the church, and as such is manifested only in an attitude of individual believers. This attitude subsequently becomes the structural characteristic of the local community in which difference and even conflict within a community is recognized and tolerated in the unity of the Holy Spirit. This last aspect is particularly important for the concept. Conciliarity has its deepest roots in liturgical life. And the experience of the mysterious eucharistic communion with God is regarded as the source which made it possible for individual Christians to accept difference and conflict and to tolerate it in communion with one another.

The present conciliar process is a direct heir of this idea of conciliarity which was cherished in the ecumenical movement at the end of the 1960s and the beginning of the 1970s. However, the word 'process' has now become substantive. This word seems to have at least two important functions. One is to stress that what is being put forward is not a concept of the churches' obligation to one another, but that in a process with an open end the diversity of all participants is respected. Another function is to indicate that now the essential structure of conciliarity focussed on movement is being expressed from below in all kinds of concrete but changeable and changing forms of council.

Now if we set the conciliar process against this background, we can see a relationship of tension. To recognize this we must recall that when the term 'conciliarity' was developed, people were in search of the theological principle which made decisive and authoritative statements possible at a council. They found this theological principle within and under the fact that Christians supported one another in a brotherly and sisterly way in the early church, that one could take part in the celebrations in other local churches, that churches exchanged ministers, that there was mutual admonition on a basis of equality – in short, that there was open communication in the community. But there is unmistakably a contradiction between conciliarity depicted in an idyllic theological way, a purely theological concept – perhaps too pure a concept – on the one hand and the actual practice of conciliar gatherings on the other. The latter were, rather, meetings at which authoritative statements were made and limits were set to differences and conflict. Applied to the present conciliar process, the idea of binding together the different forms of being the church by making reciprocal covenants, step by step in a process, is in conflict with the classical idea of a council, though the original stimulus was provided by the idea of a council as a vision of expressing unity which gave direction.

In direct connection with this, attention should be drawn to another tension. This has to do with the fact that the substance of the starting point of the conciliar process, conciliarity, is formulated in such terms that realization of it brooks no delay, nor any step-by-step process. It is a radical postulate which cries out about the essential need for the union of both the divided church and the divided world. Hence the affinity with the idea of a council which speaks an authoritative and binding word to the world and the church that kept manifesting itself during and after Vancouver. The point is this: the invisible existential conciliarity which is presupposed is a postulate in the light of reality. But it is not a purely human postulate, and it is not just contingent. It points to a divine foundation and thus has a non-contingent legitimation. One might call this the divine 'encounter' which emerges in the 'encounter' with suffering and divided humankind. Thus conciliarity qualifies the present time as an almost eschatological time: conciliarity must take form in the world and the church now. Otherwise the claim of its presence in the mystery of the church becomes a scandal. But in this, at the same time the fact remains that this postulate cannot be realized in reality. For 'the process' deliberately does not set out to provide any model for a radically decisive and authoritative word.

Here in fact we find a variant of a painful ecumenical dilemma which keeps cropping up. This dilemma is in the first place specific to a perspective in which churches look at the nature of 'the' churches and contrast this with reality: in such a way they indicate as a norm that the obligation indicated does not allow any delay. But at the same time it is evident that realization is not in fact possible. As a result that talk, i.e. talk about conciliarity, can have a paralysing effect, so that the logical (and psychological) outcome can be loss of hope and the onset of indifference.

Is what has been said above an occasion for dropping the term 'conciliar process'? Perhaps there is something of that in the Catholic church and the Orthodox churches. In that case we must realize that above all as a result of the involvement of Orthodox theologians in the ecumenical movement the insight has penetrated that conciliarity is rooted in the eucharistic community. However, the Catholic and Orthodox view of the sacrament entails that the invisible element of conciliarity presupposed lies embedded in the visible actions and signs of priests and believers. Put in the simplest of terms, this means that any talk of conciliarity and conciliar process presupposes a visible eucharistic community. Any talk in which derivations of the word 'council' are to be found thus points to a clearly perceptible form of a realized unity.

It must be said that this view is almost self-evident. For it contains the correct intuition that talking in a pure, ideal language – as about conciliarity – is either meaningless or must already in part be reality. In addition, however, this view has the great advantage of freeing the process which is in fact taking place from the tyranny of the postulate which demands everything and from the paralysis of the action of believers which inevitably follows from it.

II. Should the concept be dropped?

However, if the disappearance of the term 'conciliar process' meant the disappearance of its content, then the disadvantages would be greater. That would be a blow to reflection on the forms of the church in and through injustice, violence and a world sorely tried by the pollution of the environment. Particularly so far as the Western church is concerned it would be a confirmation of a loss of real Christian relevance. That can be illustrated from a truly 'Roman'-Catholic reaction to the conciliar process.

In October 1989, *The Ecumenical Review*, the house journal of the World Council of Churches, published a number of articles by way of preparation for the international meeting in Seoul. One of the articles was entitled 'The JIPC Process. A Catholic Contribution'. However, reading this article makes one question whether the title is correct. For if one relates the image of the church which appears in it to the theme of 'the process', it becomes clear that there is a marked contradiction between this image of the church and the intentions of 'the process'.

The first thing that strikes one is that the words which sum up the whole theme of the conciliar process are 'peace' and 'harmony'. It is no chance, moreover, that the document puts the term 'peace' first and not the term 'justice'. The schema of the text is further determined by the idea that peace and harmony are already given to the world, specifically by the exclusive initiative of the triune God (especially 1, 9, 11, 12). The concrete significance of this is that we human beings do not need to create this peace, but that we need only to draw on the source which is already given and which continually streams forth (13, 15, 18). If we have a share in this peace, justice and the conservation of nature also become possible.

According to the article, the church is the sacrament of this peace which has already been given, the sacrament of the 'intimate union of humankind with God and of the unity of all humankind' (1). Here the text conveys the impression that just as peace is given beforehand by the triune God, so the church in its turn to some degree controls this peace as a static given and presents it to the world. The horizon of experience within which the text lives is therefore the conviction of faith that what the world is really striving for, i.e. the reconciled state of an all-embracing peace, is really always already present through the church in a sacramental, objectified form. So the document begins from a church which is first separate from the world and then turns to the world. This is confirmed by its view of sin. The world, described in theological terms as creation, is subject to sin (15). However, this sin – the deepest root of which is personal sin, from which structural sin flows – does not affect the church. For the church is given the capacity to remind humankind of its calling to peace (2); the church, this 'expert in humanity' (31), makes each individual aware of his or her personal responsibility and the duty of universal solidarity. The crisis in which the world finds itself is, moreover, most deeply a religious and ethical crisis of the individual disposition. Hence in the face of hatred, threats, violence and discrimination the church must introduce new feelings into human spirits, feelings which generate a peace that is fully inspired by the gospel of peace (20). So the summons goes out from the church to the world in a unilinear way. Only once does the text contain an appeal for the renewal of the church, and on closer inspection that seems to be a renewal of the call to conversion (18); evidently because human sin constantly takes on new forms.

This view is so familiar that we may overlook the fact that it is disastrous to the original dynamic of the conciliar process. To mention just a few points:

There is for example the call to solidarity from above. This call must inevitably be frustrated. For solidarity can never be presented from above as a duty, not even if it is presented as the real calling of men and women. And certainly not if that happens through an institution which itself has a hierarchical structure.

Secondly, there is the view of the obligations of individual Christians. The text speaks *ad nauseam* about the duty of the commitment of individual Christians and organizations to peace – described in religious terms (and in addition also about the concrete struggle for justice and the conservation of nature). This duty flows from the nature of the faith which is alive in the church. But precisely because there is such a strict division between church and world, this duty cannot be said to be essential in the sphere where Christians and churches also already make up part of the divided world. From the perspective of 'the world', this is simply a purely external obligation. A priori, the term 'church' has usurped the term 'world' and in the first instance given it a negative qualification. As a result of this, a signal can never come from the divided world which is not *a priori* already integrated into the self-image of the church.

As a result, the document can leave an after-taste of the complete certainty of the 'church triumphant' which is now already in existence and thus also the suspicion that when Christians commit themselves to the world, they do so against the background of the thought that in the last instance reconciliation has already been realized in the church; and that even where the church does not accept the peace that is offered, there can be no ultimate disappointment, for there is always the church as a refuge, as a last sanctuary. Therefore the ethical problem has no true and intrinsic theological force. This is a presupposition from which the conciliar process departed. This typically *Roman* Catholic text does not recognize any 'necessity for a council' urged on it by the divided world.

And what about the call to the churches to enter into an alliance? On that point the article is just as disappointing. It refers to the well-known article 12 of the Vatican II decree *Unitatis Redingratio*. And it interprets that article in such a way that there is a *possibility* of the collaboration of churches (1). But the article is in fact silent about the necessity which has emerged from the needs of the world situation for the churches to commit themselves to one another. In the end we are given the impression that the needs of the world do not have any intrinsic significance for the necessity for an authentic Christian ecumene of churches, whereas these needs were an important element in the commitment of the appeal to the conciliar process. That appeal in fact called for a bond of conciliarity, and thus the tradition of striving for church unity and service to the world.

III. Towards a living ecclesiology?

One of the positive outcomes of the discussions over the conciliar process is that almost all the churches are agreed that Christian faith in the one creator God and Christian trust in the human community created by Christ through the Spirit make it obvious that the church must counter the threats to peace, justice and the integrity of creation. There need be no further discussion of this fundamental assumption. It is generally evident that the church is not betraying its mission and task if it is occupied with the theme of the conciliar process. But after this common recognition, of course a number of problems remain. My impression is that one of the most far-reaching of them is the question whether there can really be said to be a 'necessity for a council' arising out of the situation of the riven world: can we talk of a really decisive crisis, such that the *kairos* for the holding of a new form of conciliar discussion has dawned? This question, or rather this complex of questions, depends on the answer given to the question often posed in the ecumenical movement as to the relationship between the unity of the church and the unity of humankind.

To explain that briefly, I have to simplify things and to divide the many existing ecclesiologies roughly into two types: (a) those which tend towards a sacral-objectified presence of Jesus Christ in the church and from this overflowing source commit themselves to the unity of divided humankind (see section 2 above, the familiar Catholic view), and (b) the type which tends to see the nature of the church as an eschatological assembly from which the task of a prophetic criticism issues. Now it is important to see that on close examination not just the first type, but neither type, is in a position to recognize a crisis and *kairos* which is determined by a specific historical context. Both lack the capacity to do this. That is more than clear in the first type. For in the last instance this type points to the salvation which is always already given from eternity, which is not essentially under threat from the fate of the world. Things are different with the second type. The point is that, precisely because here the nature of the church is interpreted *a priori* as eschatological, the church always has the task of prophetic criticism. From this perspective the world is always in crisis, so every moment is a moment of crisis. And the church is *a priori* called to prophetic authority. As a result, here too no specific moment which can be localized in history can exist at which there is talk of the 'necessity for a council'. This type can be seen above all where the term 'conciliarity' is regarded as an existential of the church (see above, under 1).

So despite all the great differences between the two types of ecclesiology, they do have one thing in common: the experiential context from which they reflect on their mission and task towards the unity of the world and thus towards justice, peace and integrity *initially* lies exclusively in a separate Christian sphere of the world. In the first case this is more in the eucharistic experience within the church; in the second, it is more in the eschatological experience which occurs through the prophetic word of God which is proclaimed by the church.[2]

But precisely this division between the church or the Christian proclamation of the word on the one hand (both in terms of what has essentially been formulated) and the world on the other is extremely problematical.[3] This division – which moreover perhaps has more to do with the social process of differentiation of a Western society in the process of modernization than with so-called specifically theological foundations –

has already been recognized and criticized by a large number of theologians. The saying of Ernst Lange that what divides the world also divides the church is well known. The conflicts which dominate the world are thus also to be found in the furthest, most spiritual corners of the churches. This means that only a theological and religious sensibility which is aware of the interaction between the mysterious anticipation of salvation in sacrament and word on the one hand and the concrete struggle and concrete conflicts on the other can provide the possibility of recognizing crisis and *kairos*, and thus at a particular moment in history be able to say that the situation in the world is such as to indicate the 'necessity for a council'.

What we have here is a religious and theological sensibility which on the one hand cannot give a theological interpretation of conflicts, struggle and suffering in advance, in church terms, or through preaching, yet which on the other hand succeeds in giving a theological significance to these conflicts, this struggle and that suffering. Here an ecclesiology can be helpful which makes it clear that anticipation of salvation in the eucharist and the proclamation of the word can never be a genuine anticipation unless there is discipleship of Jesus and thus a real partisan choice in the conflicts. This will presumably be an ecclesiology which puts a stronger accent on the event of the Spirit than on the christological foundation of the church, precisely because through that event of the Spirit there are more possibilities of indicating God's presence in the world. But above all we need an ecclesiology in which there is a sense that joy over the reality of the risen Christ is never a static-eirenical possession of the church but is possible only when the church participates in the struggle of those who suffer from the devastations of the unjust, the violent and the exploiters. For only then is there a possibility of seeing the *kairos* which arises when the God of life is essentially threatened by the death of injustice, violence and annihilation.

Translated by John Bowden

Notes

1. *The Ecumenical Review* 41, 1989, 591–602. The references in the text are to the numbers in the document itself.

2. It must be mentioned that the term 'conciliarity' enjoyed great popularity in the ecumenical movement at the beginning of the 1970s precisely because it was sensed that the oppositions and conflicts in the world were playing a greater role within the existing

church than a theological definition of the church would acknowledge (on this see Ernst Lange, *Die ökumenische Utopie*, Stuttgart 1972, 177ff.). But my point here is that the term conciliarity had a tendency towards ecclesiological narrowness, because the starting point of thought about the concept is unity in difference, which is thought of as given to the church as its essence.

3. I am particularly inspired in what follows by the work of K. Raiser. See K. Raiser, 'Einheit der Kirche und Einheit der Menschheit: Überlgungen zum Thema ökumenischer Theologie', in *Ökumenische Rundschau* 35, 1986, 18–34.

B. Ecology related to Theology, Nature and Society

Ecological Perspectives in the Christian Doctrine of Creation

Alexandre Ganoczy

The environmental crisis which is now being experienced by our planetary collective is a specifically modern and post-modern phenomenon. Only in recent years has the Christian theology of creation been in a position to react to it scientifically[1] and to attempt ecological-theological statements of ethical significance.[2]

It does not have to invent everything here, for the tradition which it has to interpret contains quite a few approaches to an environmental theology which must now be discovered and actualized.

By way of an example I shall present and reflect systematically on some of these approaches here.

I. The soteriology of creation

It seems necessary to begin with that doctrine of redemption (soteriology) in which talk of creation must end up during times of crisis. Particularly today it is no longer enough to make nature, plants, animals and human beings the object of aesthetic, if not purely 'primal historical', consideration. It has become a matter of urgency to reflect on their common redemption from the perspective of faith and to reflect theologically on the possibilities of their survival and life together.

I therefore want to take the somewhat unusual approach of moving back from New Testament texts to Old Testament texts. A specifically Christian 'soteriology of creation' can first of all be derived from Romans 8. Here the creation (*ktisis*) is spoken of several times in cosmological terms (8.19, 20f., 22, 39; cf. 1.20, 25); the word 'primarily' denotes the community of creation outside humankind.[3] In so far as it 'is subject' to 'nothingness' or futility (*mataioteti*, v. 20), this suffers a 'bondage to decay' (v. 21).

Who has enslaved it? Who has so 'subjected it', this creation which was made to serve human beings, as their 'garden', that it is now in need of liberation? We human beings have. That is the answer given, among others, by Luther and Calvin. Luther thinks that creation is delivered over to the 'vanity' and the 'perverse enjoyment' of human beings.[4] And Calvin declares that 'all innocent creatures' must 'bear the penalty for our sins'.[5] Probably Paul himself thinks that human conduct and fate draw fellow creatures into a companionship of suffering, so that a common destiny comes into being between humankind and non-human nature, in which 'nature' can really become the weaker part. To put it in modern terms: the human genre becomes a burden on its environment.

Now for this society of unequals there is also hope in the positive sense. We ourselves have been 'saved for hope' (v. 24). We suffer under the eschatological 'not yet' of our salvation, and we 'groan in the expectation of sonship' (v. 23) which God has promised us. The 'revelation of the sons of God' (v. 19) and their consummation is still to come. We wait for it, along with our fellow-creatures, in longing expectation (ibid.). For it is to be expected that the fully redeemed, healed, liberated person also means 'salvation' for the cosmos – analogous but real.

Perhaps I can clarify this with the help of the rabbinic idea of the 'discipleship of God'. Human beings are called by their Creator to follow him, are called to an *imitatio Dei*. It follows from this that just as God turns in mercy to his creation, including animals and plants, so should his adopted children.[6] Accordingly if believers were complete children of God, they would behave towards the environment or towards society as God does.

Until then, however, 'The whole creation has been groaning together in pain' (v. 22),[7] probably in 'birth pangs',[8] since that symbiosis of all fellow creatures willed by God is still in an embryonic state, though for Paul it is well advanced. Be this as it may, the 'woes' involve all creatures: human beings who rule as well as creation which is enslaved.

For this reason Paul produces a whole community of fellow-groaners. Those who sigh are all creation (v. 22), the redeemed who are not yet complete (v. 23) and – presumably the decisive factor – the Spirit of God

(vv. 26f.). This Spirit intercedes for human beings with God the Father (v. 27), and in so doing certainly does not overlook their link with the environment. So the voice of the Spirit also utters a cosmic-collective cry to the liberating Creator.

However, this Spirit – with whose 'ecological' inspirations we must especially reckon today[9] – is the Spirit of Jesus Christ (v. 9), and 'the Spirit of the one who has raised Jesus from the dead' (v. 11). The triadic structure of the text is unmistakable. So it presents the divine community of life and love to the whole collective of creation as a goal.

Now does the strict christocentrism of the economy of redemption depicted here rule out any connection of the statement with the Old Testament theology of creation and its ecological implications? Not at all!

Provided that we take the theme of the image of God as a bridge, then for example Col. 3.9–10 gives us a way which ultimately leads back to Gen. 1.26–28: 'Put off the old self with its actions and put on the new self which is (continually) renewed in knowledge according to the image of its creator.'[10] The new self, which truly lives and works in the image of its creator, is Jesus the Christ. It is the image of God *par excellence* (Col. 1.15; cf. II Cor. 4.4) which the believer 'puts on' in baptism. The conformity with Christ which is meant here, and which is also ethically decisive, thus points to the conformity with God of the human creation which, according to Gen. 1.26–28, the Creator has similarly destined to be active in relation to the environment.

II. The two scenes of 'subject' and 'rule'

This follows from the close connection betweeen the two themes of Genesis, the image of God and the task of creation.[11] The former means that human beings, in two sexes, are created to be actively assimilated to the God in whose image they are. So, too, their relationship to the creatures which are their fellow-creatures should correspond to the divine conduct. If the Creator rules over his creation with blessing and concern, directing it towards autonomy (cf. Gen. 1.11ff.), freedom and prosperity, then human beings, created in his image, cannot act otherwise.

Hence a theological ecology will note the following results of Old Testament exegesis. Depending on the context, the word 'subject' (*kābaš*) has several meanings, some of which have connotations of violence and brutality,[12] for example subjecting and overthrowing enemies. However, its basic significance is neutral: 'putting a foot on an object or a living being'.[13] Now this gesture often symbolizes taking possession of, or even protection, care and concern (cf. Ps. 8.7; Josh. 18.1). Since at the command of the peaceable Creator of the Priestly Writing human beings have to set foot on the earth, the latter connotation seems much more likely than the former, violent, one which can be connected with wilful exploitation.[14]

The same is also true of the word 'rule' (*rādāh*). In view of the purely vegetarian food (Gen. 1.29f.) which the Priestly Writing envisages before the flood (cf. Gen. 9.1–3), but even more in view of the providential rule of the divine image over all living beings, any tyrannical mode of rule would probably lie outside the intention of the text. What shines through is rather the ancient Near Eastern ideal of the good and just shepherd. And this seems all the more probable, since *rādāh* also denotes the 'shepherd going round with his flock' and 'leading it to good pastures', protecting it and defending it against marauding beasts.[15]

Such a 'subjection' of the earth and such a 'rule' over the animal world are thus entrusted to the bi-sexual image of the Creator. That this ideal could really be realized only in Jesus the Christ, the new and last, i.e. eschatological, Adam, the image of God, once again simply stresses the need to think of theological ecology in christological terms. (Here one could refer to the saying of the Johannine Jesus, 'I am the good shepherd. The good shepherd gives his life for the sheep' [John 10.11], where a contrast is made with the 'hireling'. Certainly this is not an explicitly ecological logion, but 'just' a soteriological one. But given the relevance of Christian soteriology to the environment indicated above, my extended interpretation may not be completely out of place.)

What also need to be added are the caring Father's love for nature attested directly or indirectly in synoptic texts like Matt. 5.43–45; 6.25–35; 10.29–31, which embraces plants, animals and human beings; the parables of Jesus which exalt nature to be a 'preacher of the kingly rule of God';[16] and finally the Spirit of God in whose power Jesus drives out demons (Matt. 12.28), in order also to indicate the ecologically relevant triad of creation at the level of Jesus.

III. Patristic testimonies

Now it could be asked whether the post-biblical tradition, say that of the Fathers and the mediaeval theologians, changed or even distorted this position.

Research show that the Fathers largely advocated two theses: (*a*) human beings forfeited the 'dominion of the earth' through the fall; (*b*) they continue to possess it despite the fall.[17] The first thesis markedly reduces the ecological scope of Gen. 1.28 and replaces it with an individual-ethical, ascetic perspective: 'Man is to raise himself above the level of the beasts by self-discipline, following his understanding',[18] i.e. raise himself up again. The second thesis remains 'ecologically' open: even fallen human beings can and should rule in terms of the task entrusted to them by creation.

One constant which can be established among fathers of the most varied philosophical mould is the stress on a wisdom which is bound up with knowledge.

Human beings show themselves to be lords over all non-human creatures by having been given wisdom. This allows them not only to have a right understanding of God, but at the same time to observe the course of the stars, to build cities, discover laws and medicine,[19] and consequently achieve a quite definite, firm, active relationship to the world.

According to Lactantius, it is certain that the world was made by God with the aim that human beings should come into being to recognize their Creator and enjoy his good things.[20] To this end they seek out and use fire, water, earth, mountains, seas – just the things that they need to be able to engage in economic activity.[21] Thus human beings prove, as Eusebius puts it, to be 'offshoots of the divine reason' and the 'only rational race capable of the love of God' among all their fellow creatures.[22] To this degree, at least, human beings can see themselves as living beings in the image of their Creator, when they can combine knowledge with wisdom.[23]

Divine providence certainly cares primarily for human beings. But Origen stresses against the Gnostic Celsus that the same providence would 'logically also benefit the being without reason'.[24] In so doing he puts a new emphasis on Jesus' words which bring human beings, animals and plants together under the one providence of the Father. The 'environment' can no more be a matter of indifference to the image of God than it can be to God himself.

With Augustine, this theological-ecological perspective is enriched with a soteriological dimension. First of all, the Bishop of Hippo stresses that the creation outside human beings, whether animate or inanimate, has more than just 'utilitarian value'. It is not exclusively there to satisfy human needs. Rather, reason assigns it an 'objectively given rank' in the hierarchy of being.[25] Very much in line with Rom. 8, where non-human creatures join in the sighing, Augustine also sees 'flaws' in creation. However, unlike human beings, these creatures have committed no offence. Even after the fall they retain 'the goodness of their natures'. [26]

The sinner in particular must constantly take to heart this latter goodness and see the goodness that the Creator 'has guaranteed and still guarantees' in the depth of the human creation itself. Sinners are to kindle reason, 'the divine spark', within themselves, in such a way that inventions, science, knowledge of heaven and earth, technology, the building of machines, art and any kind of work are used not only in the service of healing but also in that of salvation, despite the ambivalence and danger which attach to them because of sinfulness.[27] In this connection Augustine significantly quotes Rom. 8.32: God 'did not spare his own Son but gave him up for all of us. How should he not give us all things together with him?' The saving act of the Creator, addressed in this way, certainly relates above all to human salvation, but it also takes in the material nature already in our body, which one day will be a 'spiritual' body. In a christological and implicitly trinitarian way, healing and salvation are connected with the 'environment', so that reason as an effective gift of God is called into action.

My short survey of patristic witnesses shows adequately that here work is elevated into a theological factor. Work somehow makes us like God. There is something like an *analogia laboris* between the Creator and his creative image.

Among other things, Stoic influence can be detected behind this, alongside rabbinic thought, according to which work, like the sabbath, is a command of Yahweh.[28] However, the Pauline work ethic, too, is not remote from this: true Christians do not merely value craftsmanship highly (cf. II Thess. 3.10), but also know that when they are active in an apostolic way they are fellow workers with God (I Cor. 3.9; II Cor. 6.1).

It would certainly be wrong and anachronistic to extract a regular ecological doctrine of creation and salvation from the patristic tradition. Its anthropocentrism[29] is indisputable. There is still no secular science associated with it, to set the evolutionary and other kinds of involvement in matter of *homo sapiens et faber* alongside theological anthropology. Nevertheless, certain new interpretations of the biblical task of creation and the understanding of the cosmos grounded in Christ can be demonstrated in it.

IV. Ecological wisdom in the Middle Ages

These traces are not lost in the mediaeval theology of creation, either in theory or in practice.

Reference should first be made to the Benedictine and Cistercian work ethic as the living out of belief in creation. The rule of Benedict of Nursia is governed by the famous slogan *ora et labora*, 'pray and work'.

It holds (ch. 48) that 'idleness is the enemy of the soul' and makes agricultural work and craft a correlate to liturgical and contemplative worship. What gives work meaning is not the exploitation of nature, far less the quest for profit, but producing culture. In addition there is that social bent which finds special expression in the hospitality of the monastery,[30] and therefore something that nowadays we could call 'social ecology'. Accordingly a relatively new ideal of holiness took shape at that time, which includes 'cultivating the land'[31] alongside love of God and neighbour and asceticism as the decisive virtues. So agriculture, craft and technology could once again be tied into the life of faith which controlled them.

The Cistercians who revived Benedict's rule in the twelfth century were pioneers in technical innovations. As an example I just quote a contemporary description of the monastery of Clairvaux in which the stream flowing through its countryside is as it were personified. It 'looks out everywhere' to see how its 'services' can be offered to some purpose, 'whether for cooking, sewing, crushing, irrigating, washing or grinding'. It does not 'refuse' any task.[32] Here part of the environment is quite lovingly drawn into the great service of culture. And that happens in a spirit for which human creation can and should contain the value of a responsible continuation of the divine work of creation.[33] This view also contains an eschatological element, for example according to the mediaeval motto *renovatio in melius*. The Christian who creates a culture which does justice to the environment is performing a service for the coming rule of God.[34]

In Hugo of St Victor we have a significant witness to that mediaeval understanding of nature which could make both the animal and the machine the objects of the responsibility of faith. God wants human beings not only to dominate and use the animal world but also to care for it and acquire the necessary knowledge: 'God leaves to human beings the care of oxen and other animals so that they are subject to their rule and are dominated by their reason, so that they can also know what needs to be done for those from whom they receive obedience.'[35]

On the other hand, the same Hugo argues that mechanics should be incorporated into the study of philosophy as the fourth 'art'. Now this discipline has its model in the world of nature and in its 'machine' created by God. It is to direct itself in accordance with this. The implements devised by human beings must follow the divine invention and thus be used as instruments for the fulfilment of the task of creation.[36] The idea of a technology with an ecological norm is close.

V. No 'back to nature' in modernity

The narrow limits of this article make it impossible to go into the difficult question from what point Christians began to understand Gen. 1.28 as *carte blanche* to exploit the environment. There is much to point to an anthropocentricism in Renaissance humanism, initially lauded poetically and then imposed inexorably, in which the real theological and christological roots of belief in creation as found in Rom. 8 and Col. 3 were strongly repressed. To mkae Descartes the scapegoat for an ice-cold mathematical objectification of plants, animals and matter under the tyranny of the *res cogitans* seems to be an undertaking which has hardly any basis in the texts of the philosopher. To do him justice, one must not just keep citing those texts, torn from their context, in which he calls human beings 'maîtres et possesseurs de la nature' (*Discourse* VI.62) and compares organisms with machines (*Meditations* VI.33), but must also bring those instances in which Descartes makes clear the innermost correlation between the world of subject and object, for example through the body, in which 'I am not just present in the same way as the sailor in his vessel' (*Meditations* VI.26).

At all events, no modern ecological ethic can go back behind the scientific thinking which left a decisive mark on Descartes. There can be no 'back to nature' in the Romantic or animistic sense. Rather, Christians have to use all the achievements of modern science and technology in accordance with the task of creation and the 'rule of the shepherd' associated with it, so that their soteriological service does not by-pass reality.

Granted, this is a personal view,[37] but it does claim to re-mint the beginnings of a theology of creation made at Vatican II, though it has to be conceded that an ecological awareness was still almost completely absent there.

VI. An ecological theology?

It is certainly not simple to find ecological beginnings in the conciliar theology of creation. The Pastoral Constitution *Gaudium et Spes*, in which these might have been expected, given its subject-matter, is at first largely disappointing. The problems of the destruction of the environment, the extermination of whole species, an earth which is getting increasingly uninhabitable, are not mentioned anywhere. There seem to be only two statements which suggest a human responsibility for non-human creation.

The first relates to the 'autonomy of earthly realities' which is bound up with the recognition in faith that through the 'will of the Creator', the 'individual realities' have their 'own goodness' and their autonomy and their own orders.

The second introduces a soteriological note: 'Redeemed by Christ and made a new creature by the Holy Spirit, man can, indeed he must, love the things of God's creation' (37.4).

Some lines before this passage, 'disordered love of self' is addressed as a danger to 'human creativity'. Would it not have been appropriate to censure the consequences of this self-love which are destroying the environment? Instead of this, the Constitution talks with an anthropocentrism which already sounds somewhat naive to our ears. Thus without any warning, in connection with Gen. 1.26–28 there is stress only on the conquest of the earth 'with all it contains' (34.1; cf. 63.2; 65.1). It is also added that 'victories of mankind are a sign of the greatness of God', without sparing a word for the catastrophic price which nature has to pay for human victories in, say, the economic sphere.

An implicitly ecological theology emerges only from the *dogmatic* statements in *Gaudium et Spes*. No. 22 already introduces the message of Rom. 8 and Col. 1–3 which I expounded at the beginning. Only in Christ as the one true image of God is the 'mystery of humanity' manifest. Only it can so restore in us the image of the Creator, through his Spirit, that human beings are associated with 'the redemptive work of Jesus Christ himself through the homage of work offered to God' (67.2).

Thus the Pauline-mediaeval work-ethic is put in an appropriate context. Jesus 'worked with human hands' (22.2; cf. 43.1; 67.2), and in so doing already showed the way in which our activity can further develop (*evolvere*) (34.2) the work of the Creator and indeed bring it to 'completion' (57.2; 67.2). Otherwise it easily degenerates into an 'instrument of sin' (37.3); I would add that this is a daily sin against the environment.

VII. Conclusion

In conclusion, I would venture the following verdict. Certainly Vatican II is far from taking account of all the ecological implications of the Christian tradition of faith. Nevertheless, it makes an essential contribution in developing its talk of human creativity in the framework of a soteriology related to action, which has both christocentric and trinitarian dimensions.

Here at all events we can grasp one constant of the tradition. In the

Christian understanding of faith, the crisis cannot be overcome under the slogan 'back to nature'; it must be overcome, rather, through a redemptive use of all the achievements of science and technology. In the steps of God the Christian should walk as the good and inventive shepherd of nature. In this connection one might also read the so-called 'Basle Document' of the European Assembly, *Peace in Justice*.[38]

Translated by John Bowden

Notes

1. This has been stimulated in the German-speaking world by thinkers like C. F. von Weizsäcker, G. Picht, A. M. Klaus Müller, G. Altner, J. Moltmann, and others.
2. See A. Ganoczy, 'Ökologie', *Lexikon der katholischen Dogmatik*, Freiburg, etc. 1987, 395f.
3. Cf. U. Wilckens, *Der Brief an die Römer*, EKK VI.2, Zurich etc. 1980, 153.
4. Cf. the 1515/16 lectures on Romans, Latin/German edition II, Darmstadt 1960, 98–102.
5. *Comm. in Ep. ad Rom.* 8.21, OC 48–49, 153; cf. *Institutio* III 25.2.
6. Cf. A. Nissen, *Gott und der Nächste im antiken Judentum. Untersuchungen zum Doppelgebot der Liebe*, Tübingen 1974, 70–5; see also 278–86.
7. See (W. Bauer), W. F. Arndt, F. W. Gingrich and F. W. Danker, *Lexicon of New Testament Greek*, Chicago ²1979, 793, s.v. *synodino*.
8. Ibid., and L. Schottroff, *Schöpfung im Neuen Testament*; G. Altner (ed.), *Okologische Theologie. Perspectiven zur Orientierung*, Stuttgart 1989, 130–48.
9. Cf. Wilckens, *Römer* (n.3), 136. A reference to Gal. 5.18: the spirit 'leads' (rather than 'drives').
10. E. Schweizer, *Der Brief an die Kolosser*, EKK, Zurich etc. 1976, 137.
11. Cf. O. H. Steck, *Der Schöpfungsbericht der Priesterschrift*, Göttingen 1975, 152; A. Ganoczy, *Schöpfungslehre*, Düsseldorf ²1987, 28–31.
12. G. Liedke, 'Von der Ausbeutung zur Ko-operation. Theologisch-philosophische Überlegungen zum Problem des Umweltschutzes', in E. von Weizsäcker (ed.), *Humanökologie und Umweltschutz*, Stuttgart and Munich 1972, 36–65: 44.
13. E. Zenger, *Der Gott der Bibel*, Stuttgart ²1981, 148.
14. For the whole of this discussion see N. Lohfink, '"Macht euch die Erde untertan"?', *Orientierung* 38, 1974, 137–42.
15. Zenger, *Gott der Bibel* (n.13), 149.
16. G. Bornkamm, *Jesus of Nazareth*, London and New York 1960, 118.
17. U. Krolzik, *Umweltkrise – Folge des Christentums?*, Stuttgart and Berlin 1979, 73: instances 109.
18. Ibid., 73f.
19. Thus for example the *Pseudo-Clementine Homilies* III, 36, GCS 42, 69f.
20. *Epitome divinarum institutionum* 63–5; CSEL 19, 750–5.
21. *De ira dei* 13.1–2 [ed. H. Kraft and A. Wlosok], Darmstadt 1957, 42f.

22. *Theophania* I, 44–7: GCS 11.1–2, 61–62.
23. Ibid.
24. *Contra Celsum* IV.74; PG 11, 1143–46.
25. *De civitate Dei* XI.16, PL 41,336.
26. Ibid., XII.4: PL 41, 351f.
27. Ibid., XXIII, 24; PL 41, 788–92.
28. Cf. Krolzik, *Umweltkrise* (n.17), 63.
29. For this theme see A. Auer, *Umweltethik. Ein theologischer Beitrag zur ökologischen Diskussion*, Düsseldorf 1984, 54–64, 203–22.
30. Cf. A. Blazovich, *Soziologie des Mönchtums und der Benediktinerregel*, Vienna 1954.
31. Cf. K. Weber, 'Kulturgeschichtliche Probleme der Merowingerzeit im Spiegel frühmittelalterlicher Heiligenleben', in *Studien und Mitteilungen zur Geschichte des Benediktinerordens* 48, 1930, 349–51.
32. *Descriptio positionis seu situationis monasterii Clarae-Vallensis*, PL 185, 570f.
33. Cf. J. Leclercq, *L'amour des lettres et le désir de Dieu. Initiation aux auteurs monastiques du Moyen Age*, Paris 1957.
34. Krolzik, *Umweltkrise* (n.17), 69.
35. *De sacramentis* I, 6.13; PL 176, 271; quoted in Krolzik, *Umweltkrise* (n.17), 77.
36. *De arca Noe morali* IV. 6; PL 176, 672; quoted in Krolzik, *Umweltkrise* (n.17), 79.
37. Cf. A. Ganoczy, *Theologie der Natur*, Zurich, etc. 1982.
38. *Europäische ökumenische Versammlung Frieden in Gerechtigkeit. Basel 15.–21. Mai 1989. Das Document* (edited by the Secretariat of the German Bishops' Conference), Arbeitshilfen 70, Bonn 1989.

The Community of Creation as a Community in Law. The New Contract between the Generations

Günter Altner

I. Creatures among other creatures

The faith in creation stimulated by the biblical tradition and the responsibility for creation connected with it have no ontological structure. Here there is no hierarchy of duties which would simply correspond to the hierarchical structure of inanimate and inanimate reality. Creation is an event in time, a dynamic of becoming, from which human beings emerge and in which they find themselves involved. They are therefore creatures among other creatures. Their special position rests on the fact that they share in God's knowledge. In human beings, creation becomes conscious of itself, and the mystery of its origin, which creation needs at every moment of its becoming, is reflected in this consciousness. To this degree, as those who share knowledge, human beings are more deeply and more radically involved in the event of creation than can be true of any other creature. They are aware of the love which goes out to all creation and from which all creation lives, and from this awareness there grows in them a capacity for and obligation to their fellow human beings and their fellow creatures.

If we take this view, first of all we are completely free from the dualism between the protection of human beings and the protection of creation which has become so highly stylized today. In that case human beings are also free from all self-definitions (human beings as flawed beings, as beings who are aware of themselves) and all the hierarchies of values over against the animal and plant kingdoms which are to be derived from them. The prime obligation of human beings towards their fellow creatures does not derive from the existence of self-awareness, sensitivity to pain and any special human achievements, but from the knowledge of the goodness of all creation, which communicates itself through the process of creation. In short, nature imposes values because it is creation. This recognition also includes insight into the manifold variety of creatures and the acknowledgment of future generations in the course of the general process of the coming into being of creation.

II. The protection of human beings or the protection of animals?

H. Ruh has argued that the Bible puts forward a relatively pragmatic view of the conflict between the interests (or rights) of human beings and those of animals to life: 'For all the stress on the minimizing of suffering to animals, our starting point can be that in the case of a conflict between the severe suffering of human beings and that of animals, in any particular instance human beings can be given priority, because the biblical evidence as a whole takes human intervention in the animal world almost as a matter of course – within restricted limits. In this perspective, researchers who justify the need for animal experiments with an appeal to the divine command therefore have good arguments on their side.'[1]

If there were no deep reflection in the Bible on a primal state of creation in which human beings did not eat meat, and if there were not also those statements about a future peace which embraces human beings and all creatures, and finally if there were no witness in the New Testament to that radical message of the non-violent surrender of love to the world, then we would have to concede that Ruh was right. But that is not the case. The biblical tradition offers us a picture of a world which has taken reverence for life seriously and which is therefore transparent to the deeper goodness of all creation. The primary element is the praise of creation and its Creator and not the way in which human beings define themselves towards creation.

The philosophical discussion about the protection of animals and human beings which is being carried on so intensively today is taking quite a different course. In it, arguments essentially revolve round the question how far there can be any question of an identity of interests between human beings and animals. Here H. F. Kaplan has adopted the most complex approach. By listing a comprehensive number of common features in animal and human experience he has come to the conclusion that animals and human beings do have common interests. This finding then becomes the basis for the formulation of the principle of equality: 'The similar interests of living beings whose experiences can be causally influenced directly or in principle by our actions should play the same role in the moral considerations which underlie our actions, i.e. should determine our actions to the same degree.'[2] Here the well-being of the rest of creation is ethically relevant only to the degree that is comparable to the existential interests of human beings or can be derived from them. That is in contradiction to the general quality of the creaturely world which is derived from the notion of creation.

Of the group of philosophers whose arguments are anthropocentric, the position of Klaus M. Meyer-Abich stands out particularly clearly. He mentions essentially two criteria according to which non-human beings are worth protecting: their equality with human beings in that they belong to the universal history of nature, and in that they have an interest in wanting to have life. Although the starting point here is comparability with human beings, human beings are not the focal point of the argument. Rather, the argument revolves round the fact that all creatures (including human beings) have a share in the history of nature and the intentionality of all life. Because life is something that all creatures have, it is experienced in different ways as something worth maintaining.

In this connection, Meyer-Abich goes even beyond animate nature: 'With animals and plants, with earth, water, air and fire, humankind emerged from the history of nature as one among millions of genres on the tree of life . . . Now this affinity brings with it similarities on the basis of which, in theory, the principle of equality can be applied to the relationship between humankind and our natural environment.'[3] Meyer-Abich's argument does not begin with the ordered conceptual world of the human subject, however that may have been defined, but with the softer knowledge that all life is conditioned by the history of nature.

III. 'Reverence for life'

This standpoint has points of contact with the principles of a comprehensive responsibility for creation which I have developed. The living world which supports human beings and which confronts them proves to be something meaningful and worth protecting, regardless of the level and complexity of existing forms of nature. The perception that there is a deeper way in which living beings are not at the disposal of human beings and the wealth of life history, forms of life and equilibria in life transcends the possibilities of definition of a rationality which seeks to provide a basis for itself. The human self as the authority responsible for an ethic which includes non-human creation sees itself in the context of a complex coming-to-be which it has not brought about itself, but which is entrusted to it. It can, however, shape and alter this complex in one way or another, depending on its attitude. If we include all stages of the history of nature, all the phenomena of human life, and also take into account the right to life of coming generations, that means that there is no life which does not deserve to live. Any attempt to draw a line between life which does deserve to live and life which does not ultimate derives from the arbitrariness of a claim which seeks to define itself without taking into account the overall setting of life in which it exists.

If the human consciousness can be understood as part of a wider context – as Albert Schweitzer also thought – the dualism between human beings and nature which was transported into the present through scientific and technical rationality begins to break up in favour of more complex forms of discourse and activity. The forms of discourse and communication which thus become possible are an expression of a contract between the generations which is slowly coming into awareness.

IV. 'Optimal compromise'

Now if it is the case that a growing number of people understand human beings as part of a wider complex of natural history – in contrast to the anthropocentric approach, which separates human beings from nature – and if they see this as something like a guarantee of the meaning of human existence and indeed of the history of nature as a whole, we have a direct contact with the understanding of creation as a process of coming-to-be in the world which I have stressed. In this perspective, creation is an event in the world, a dynamic of coming-to-be, a sequence of generations, in which human beings find that they have a place. So human beings are creatures among other creatures – finite, mortal and transitory, like all life.

However, human beings know that they must die, and this knowledge gives them a share in the knowledge of the Creator. That is the basis of their special position. They are interested in the origin and determination of things. In human beings, creation becomes aware of its coming-to-be. So human consciousness is a reflection of the mystery of its origin, which the creation needs at every moment of its coming-to-be. To this degree, as those who share in the knowledge of the Creator, human beings are more deeply and more radically involved in the event of creation than can be true of any other creature. And that is ultimately connected with their capacity for responsibility, for attempting to make a response to the promise of meaning which encounters them in their consciousness.

If we seek to characterize this responsibility in terms of the present state of the contemporary evolutionary picture of the world, we could follow the biologist G. Strey, who remarks: 'A reckless struggle of each against all is inconceivable, and so is a sheer altruism . . . But in turn that means that what we have is a network of relationships and reciprocal dependencies, which are bound together in this network only through reciprocal support and tolerance. So here too the term "optimal compromise" seems to me the one which best describes the situation.'[4]

Here the key phrase is 'optimal compromise', which Strey on the one hand sees already realized in part in phylogeny before human beings, and on the other, from a future perspective, regards as 'the' task for coming generations. In incorporating this dimension of phylogeny into ethical considerations my view has points of contact with that of Strey, and there is also a parallel in that responsibility for creation is a genuine task for human beings which cannot be read off nature, and which today is to be related to the whole complex of life on earth (the biosphere).

V. Specific instances

How do we give specific examples of the criteria for actions which I have sketched out above in general terms and indicate relevant areas for action? Here we find a wide range of principles and rules.

1. All life is an event in time, transitory, finite and once-for-all. All human concern has to be directed towards preserving life. Here a distinction needs to be made between the right of species (plants, animals, human beings) to life and the living room and right to life which are needed by individuals (human beings and animals).

2. The recognition of the rights of non-human nature may not lead to the relativization of any stage of human existence or the denial of rights to it. Rightly understood, the extension of guarantees in law to non-human forms of life also means more thorough legal guarantees for any facet of human life (growing human life, sick human life, dying human life).

3. Human history and the history of nature are part of a comprehensive process. The rapid dynamic of human history is threatening to tear apart the indispensable ties which bind us to the history of nature, which runs more slowly. For this reason, moratoria (pause for thought) are indispensable, so that we can examine the unforeseeable consequences of science, technology and progress. For such moratoria to be regulated there is need

for a democratically legitimated process of institution and control with the participation of the critical public.

4. The present guarantee for the future history of life is the multiplicity of the species which have come into being and the interplay of their biotopes. A spirituality of creation which does not pay heed to any species is eyewash. There are no superfluous species. Without a knowledge of the species and their interplay there can be no respect for life and no guarantee of the existence of future generations. All measures which reduce the density of species (e.g. over-population, an intensification of the infrastructure, and extension of built-up areas, over-use, poisoning) need to be examined, controlled and in some cases reduced. Methods used so far to protect species, nature and biotopes are completely unsatisfactory, and in the future must be substantially strengthened in opposition to the interests of policies of trade, agriculture, industrialization and community.

5. One special problem is posed by the possibilities of intervention provided by modern biotechnology, especially gene technology and the biology of procreation. If living beings have a right to life and to procreation in line with their species, interference with heredity and the reprogramming which that produces is extremely problematical.

6. The rights of nature that are to be called for make it quite essential that the whole sphere of the use of organisms (animals and plants) should be subjected to a critical survey. Here we have on the one hand the question of a proper preservation and procreation of species. And on the other hand there must be a discussion of the function of animals as a source of food and as potential material for medical and consumer experiments (e.g. in connection with cosmetics).

7. Admonitions about the rights of nature will remain ineffective and peripheral unless at the same time they are also understood as a challenge to any technological approach and to any policy about technology. Ethical and legal reflection starts too late if it bears only on the capacity of the environment to bear technologies which already exist or are already developed.

8. There must be an end to the undervaluation of nature in theoretical and practical calculations which regard it as a resource that is available more or less freely. The rights of nature must be shaped in such a way that nature is taken seriously as a 'third partner' in business alongside labour and capital.

9. A limit is put to human existence by the biosphere as the extreme framework for human action. However, this limit remains variable depending on what demands are made on it. As is well known, Hermann

Kahn had a very optimistic view of the area available for human settlement because he began from the possibility, among others, of covering over parts of the ocean with terraces. Rights can be given successfully to nature only if this intention permeates all realms of law and levels of structure within the biosphere, from local government regulations through state constitutional law to international law.

VI. The rights of future generations

Specifically in connection with these last arguments, the 'Berne Draft Resolution', which attempts to prescribe the rights of future generations and the rights of nature, is helpful and takes us further.[5] Among the rights of future generations are listed the following:

1. Future generations have a right to life.
2. Future generations have a right not to be manipulated, i.e. to have a heredity which has not been artificially changed by human beings.
3. Future generations have a right to a varied world of plants and animals, and thus to life in a rich nature with the preservation of an abundance of genetic resources.
4. Future generations have a right to clean air, to an intact ozone layer and an adequate heat exchange between the earth and the atmosphere . . .[6]

The 'rights of nature' codified by the Berne Resolution include the following:

1. Nature – animate or inanimate – has a right to existence, i.e. to preservation and development.
2. Nature has a right to the protection of its ecosystems, and of the network of species and populations.
3. Animate nature has a right to the preservation and development of its genetic inheritance.
4. Living beings have a right to life in accordance with their species, including procreation, in the ecosystems appropriate to them.
5. Interventions in nature need to be justified . . .[7]

The lawyer Jörg Leimbacher stresses that the rights to be bestowed on nature are special rights which relate above all to its 'being there' and 'being as it is', to its state (species, populations, ecosystems) and its 'possibilities of development': 'Nature needs rights only because there are human beings, because there are human societies, because there are legal ordinances. Nature merely needs particular rights. It can dispense with freedom of the press for baobab trees or freedom of belief for turtles . . .

But if human beings threaten the existence of nature, we need to think of the right of nature to exist.'[8] The guarantees for existence which he cites (being there, being as it is, and possibilities of development) are to be understood in precisely this sense.

VII. Nature as a subject in law

On this presupposition, from the human side no intervention in nature can be treated any more as a matter of course. Here there is a need to justify human intervention in nature. There must be a demonstration of how far the consequences of intervention in nature are responsible. The limit values which have been valid so far are above all compromises between the interests of utilization and the interests of health. The important thing now is to find a way of also bringing the interests of nature, in existence and development (its interests in survival), into the equation. Here a number of questions are difficult to answer: can an interest in human utilization rate higher than the right to exist of a very rare species which occurs at only one place on earth and which would be wiped out by human settlement? For example, is it acceptable that migratory birds should lose their resting places, and thus also the possibility to exist, as a result of building by human beings?

It will be possible to resolve these and an endless series of other questions only if the law in favour of nature clearly recognizes it as part of creation. There is no way round giving nature the character of a subject in law – and thus departing from current practice. That has nothing to do with speculation about whether animals and plants have souls; it is merely a question of whether we are prepared to remove nature from the law of property – and even that would certainly be a presupposition in the spirit of a particular understanding of nature and reality – and in accordance with its nature as part of creation give it the status of a subject in law as accepted by us human beings.

Leimbacher has pointed out that 'in our legal ordinances it is possible to give rights even to a pile of money, a foundation, or to create other so-called persons in law, like joint stock companies and associations, etc.', which have their own rights as subjects in law.[9] Why should such a procedure towards nature not be both requisite and reasonable? The new feature of this process would thus not be the revolutionizing of law but the ultimate recognition by our legal system that nature has the status of a fellow creature, a status which has hitherto been withheld from it for reasons of anthropocentric prejudice. The significance of the draft Berne resolution discussed here lies not least in the fact that it expressed this clearly and succinctly.

A change in legal culture in the direction indicated here would offer a good starting point for helping the virtues of fellow-creatureliness, which over long years have been conjured up in vain, to achieve a binding character. Responsibility for creation in this sense would not then be the quotation of biblical texts for the umpteenth time but the direct involvement of human beings and nature in a legal and socially binding reciprocal relationship which would lead away from the technocratic domination of our modern age. The testimony of the Jewish–Christian tradition to creation – like the testimony of other religions to creation – is relevant for the present crisis about survival only if leads human consciousness, through a far-reaching recollection, to understand its position in the history of life in terms of the promise for coming generations inherent in that life.

As the old biblical texts of the Bible used in connection with the crisis about survival today indicate, belief in creation is knowledge of the manifold variety of life, knowledge of the common history of life, knowledge also of its infinite worth, and at the same time the ability to shape this knowledge in the direction of a new conjunction of human beings and nature – which is also binding in law. In the face of the possibility that in a changed human legal culture nature would have shares in humanity, and humanity would have shares in nature, so that the history of life became the expression of a new dimension of peace and justice – in the face of this hope, anthropocentrism remains merely the old and dangerous possibility of defining oneself over against nature. Theological and philosophical motive power in the present situation consists above all in the interplay of considerations deriving from systems theory, the theory of evolution, ecology, ethics, law and the theology of creation, in the experience of being brought into an open relationship between human beings and nature which could be the breaking-off and downfall of all that has gone before, but also a continuation on the level of a new integration.

VIII. Obstacles in the way of a community in law

At the present stage of the development of humankind, two obstacles in particular stand in the way of the realization of the community of creation as a community in law. The first is the humanist prejudice against all ecological openings in ethics, which is nurtured above all in Christian traditions. The second is the lack of any binding reason for putting this into practice. To end with I shall examine both these obstacles.

1. The conflict between an anthropocentric ethic and a biocentric ethic, or an ethic centred on creation, is characterized by all those difficulties which keep emerging when a far-reaching paradigm change takes place. Some who still maintain the old paradigm – in this case a humanistic one – can see the new attitude only as a danger to their standpoint and a relativization of it. In this connection one should point out that the realization of a community in law with creation is a genuinely human demand which does not lead to questionable patterns of assimilation to the overall complex of creatures. If we are rightly to experience nature as being made up of creatures just as we are creatures, there is need of a profoundly human achievement in the extension of humanistic categories. And this finds expression in the requirement of a legal culture in which human beings become advocates for their fellow creatures and make them legitimate legal claimants. The new element in the present situation of humanity and the crisis over survival is the way in which human categories have been opened up to the community of creation. The granting of rights to non-human creation makes the incorporation of nature into the democratic constitutional state indispensable. Just as the discussion on human rights finally – after painfully long processes of rethinking – led to the inclusion of disadvantaged groups of people in the guarantees given by the constitutional state, so today creation is standing at the doors and waiting to be admitted into the democratic constitutional state. And that brings us to the second problem barrier, the question how this process can take place as soon as possible and be made as binding as possible.

2. Since the crisis about survival is a global problem, international cooperation both from the churches (and the religions) and the states is needed if it is to be resolved. A common place of peace in Assisi is too little. More is needed here. The Berne Resolution quoted above points in the right direction. In the meantime the Berne Resolution has been approved by the executive committee of the Reformed World Alliance. In anchoring the rights of future generations and the rights of nature in human consciousness, the confessions, the churches and the religions must take the course of shared reflection. In addition we need binding declarations from the United Nations. It is almost completely unknown that as early as 1982 the General Assembly of the United Nations passed a 'World Charter for Nature'. This charter was written in the awareness 'that every form of life is unique and has a claim to be respected independently of its value for human beings, and that in order to grant this recognition to other organisms also, human beings need to be guided by a moral code of behaviour'.[10]

In future years, binding international commitments must be derived from this statement. Without such steps, talk of a community in law with creation will become cynical excuses.

Translated by John Bowden

Notes

1. H. Ruh, 'Tierrechte – Neue Folgen der Tierethik', *Zeitschrift für Evangelische Ethik* 33, 1989, 67.
2. H. F. Kaplan, *Philosophie des Vegetarismus. Kritische Würdigung und Weiterführung von Peter Singers Ansatz*, Frankfurt 1988, 94.
3. K. M. Meyer-Abich, *Wege zum Frieden mit der Natur*, Munich and Vienna 1984, 174.
4. G. Strey, *Umweltethik und Evolution*, Göttingen 1989, 81.
5. *Evengalische Theologie* 5, 1990, 434ff.
6. Ibid., 435.
7. Ibid., 436.
8. J. Leimbacher, 'Die Rechte der Natur', *Evangelische Theologie* 5, 1990, 451.
9. Ibid., 456f.
10. *Evangelische Theologie* 5, 1990, 472ff.

'The Integrity of Creation': The Third Point of the JPIC Process. Ecology between Theology and Science

Johan van Klinken

The integrity of creation, the third point in the conciliar process, implies respect for flora and fauna, and in 1990 calls urgently for a non-anthropocentric element in theology and ethics. This requirement is neither too difficult nor too remote. It concerns our planet, the present, and a concrete future within a time-span of 200 years (see 1 and 8 below, with fig. 1). Respect for all that lives can grow from religion and the sciences when biblical views[1] are rooted in the covenant and the sciences lead to overwhelming wonder (3 below). Nature and creation have been awe-inspiring at all levels of scientific insight. They have been the source and inspiration for psalms: 'How wonderful are your works, my soul knows that right well!' Such feelings remain when ecology and modern science show more clearly than ever before how marvellous the creation is in its integrity – and how vulnerable (see 7 below).

The existence of a species ranks above the rights of individual human beings or groups of human beings. The defence of all living beings (see 6 below) has priority over unlimited population growth and the reclamation of land for their use. This is a difficult message (see 8 and 9 below) for a humankind which is eager to accept the blessings of technology but turns a blind eye to ethical and religious consequences when technology becomes normative.

I. A vertical dimension

The integrity of the creation is first of all an issue with a vertical dimension.

Some value ecology and the conservation of nature as social work for the environment and wild life: this is a horizontal approach, with much of earth below, but perhaps too little of heaven above. What is urgent, however, is that churches and religions should recognize the integrity of creation as part of a vertical covenant, an intimate relationship with the Maker and what is made. Nevertheless, the integrity of creation also has horizontal ramifications: limits to human growth and consumption.

People inside and outside the churches feel in their hearts that the species have a right to exist by a higher authority than their own judgment. However, the intrinsic right of species to exist is not well expressed in most political reports[2] or debates on energy.[3] It is good that recently there has been interest in these reports and discussions, but they fall short in one important aspect, namely that they rarely rise above anthropocentric issues. Here the churches have an authentic message: flora and fauna are to be respected, not on utilitarian grounds and because of their economic potential, but on the higher level of a covenant, with the ark and the rainbow as its symbols.

Today mass extinction continues inexorably: species of plants and animals are disappearing as never before in the history of life on our planet. We have heard about it – partly by rumour, since much of the destruction of creation occurs in the depths of the seas and in remote rain-forests unknown to us. Precise numbers, if any importance is to be attached to them, are unknown, but the estimates are frightening. Here is a *cri de coeur*:

> between 1500 and 1850 one species disappeared every ten years;
> between 1850 and 1950 one species disappeared per year;
> around 1990 ten species are disappearing per day;
> around 2000 one species will disappear per hour;
> between 1975 and 2000 about twenty per cent of all species will have disappeared;
> about 2100 – we do not dare to think.

It seems as simple as it is diabolical: the more technology, the more people; the less nature, the less species, the less creation. This dying, this extinction, is not natural. It does not occur by itself, is not the result of a change in climate and certainly is not caused by the impact of meteors. It is caused by us human beings collectively. This extinction points a finger at all human beings. Perhaps we refuse to hear the accusation, but we are aware of it. And what is going to happen if, unthinkably, human beings refuse to change their behaviour, is too terrible to contemplate. Unless the biosphere is protected, this extinction may increase further after the year 2000 to fifty per cent, ninety per cent or more. It will be all holocaust.

II. A covenant against extinction

Plants and animals form part of the oldest religious testimonies: ark and rainbow in the book of Genesis, spiritual reverence in often even earlier rock paintings in various parts of the world. Human beings of all times have possessed an inner respect for nature as long as they have not been debased by standards below human dignity or enslaved by technology and consumerism. The palaeolithic hunters, the builders of megaliths in prehistoric Europe, the Masai of Africa, the city-dwellers after the industrial revolution, all lived and live in different worlds. But their feelings will not have differed much while looking at a sunset, when watching a flight of trumpeting swans in winter, when listening to the hum of bees in summer. Ecological spirituality is not beyond the hearts of Christians, but it grows more from outside than from inside the churches.

The preservation of flora and fauna has not been a topic for many theological studies, but it is now an urgent one. Fortunately the church has never been completely silent about respect for nature as part of the covenant. St Francis spoke of it;[4] the Belgic Creed spoke of it;[5] Albert Schweitzer spoke of it. But their words, their treasured words, seem no longer to be relevant in a situation which is getting out of hand. We blush for shame at the deterioration and extinction in our world when in the Apostles' Creed we name God the Father creator of heaven and earth.

We know the word 'master', we use the word 'stewardship', but the real depth lies in the word 'covenant'. 'Master' is that dangerous word from the Judaeo-Christian-Islamic tradition which is misused so as to produce slavery and oppression, while putting human beings above nature: it makes human beings the self-made judges who determine what species are beneficial and what could be wiped out. As a child of his time, René Descartes spoke the pernicious words, 'I think, and *they*, the animals and the plants, do not. *We* are the masters and can use *them* at our convenience.' Three centuries later we still feel the arrogance of these words. Through its manifold abuse, the word 'master' has become contaminated. 'Stewardship' conveys more. It can be extended to a life-centred ethics, though the word is mostly used in an anthopocentric way and often with reference to husbandry. Stewardship clearly forbids cruelty and protects animals. McDaniel puts it sympathetically: 'A recognition of our dependence on the earth can enable us to exercise that kindly use, that

non-dominating stewardship, towards which biblical traditions call us.'
'Covenant' conveys still more: we are part of the creation in a bond with all
that lives ; we 'want to live together with all Life that wants to live'. Let
these noble words of Albert Schweitzer form a worthy substitute for those
of Descartes. Where stewardship says 'no cruelty', the covenant implies 'no
extinction'.

III. Windows opened by science

Science opens windows with breathtaking views of the way in which matter
and organic life were created. It sees a history of a billions of years marked
by mysterious pathways through narrow gates with sudden turning points,
sometimes with violent death and sometimes with remarkable birth. Here
are six examples from a longer list in section 8.

1. All the matter in our bodies and in the physical world around us
consists of chemical elements. The elements were mostly formed during
the formation and collapse of early stars billions of years before the sun and
the earth were created. Without the birth and death of early stars, the earth
would not have been. Later organic life used all conceivable material
possibilities: electromagnetic waves for seeing; sound waves for hearing;
water, air and soil for an abundance of biotopes; the rhythms of day and
night, summer and winter; the magnetism of the earth utilized by
migrating birds.

2. Life requires ozone, carbon dioxide $(CO_2)^6$ and oxygen in balanced
concentrations. Too little ozone and too few ultra-violet rays destroy
organisms; too much ozone becomes poisonous. CO_2 is basic to as-
similating carbon and stabilizing the temperature of the atmosphere. The
oxygen in the air is a product of life and would disappear without the
assimilation of carbon.

3. Records of fossils show millions of species which disappeared in a
slow process of decline. By contrast, some rare catastrophes – ten to twelve
of them in the earth's histories – caused sudden extinction in a short time.
The dinosaurs were the victims of such a catastrophe sixty-six million years
ago. The extinct species failed to adjust to environmental changes. But in
that failure they made room for subsequent mammals: life through
catastrophe.

4. Genetic differentiation needs birth and death to proceed. Without
death there would be no life at all. Most species reproduce by sexual
intercourse. Without sexual intercourse the evolution would have been too
slow for life to evolve within the life-span of sun and earth. Several species

(including *homo sapiens*) survive by surplus offspring. However, this attribute for survival implies a potential for over-population when mortality is reduced without corresponding family planning.

5. The earth's orbit 'happens' to be slightly influenced by the outer planets of our solar system. That causes the occurrence of periodic ice ages and death on the northern halves of the Eurasian and American continents. At the same time the ice ages were a *conditio sine qua non* for our development.

6. The human race represents only one zoological species with minimal racial differentiation. The human child obtained an exceptionally prolonged youth for learning. The human race obtained millennia of preparation to take responsibility as collaborators with God (see 6 below).

When contemplating these points one might ask in bewilderment, 'Why?' Why did everything evolve along such surprising routes? On the one hand it looks as if these routes are accidental, while on the other they meet necessary conditions. Why these solutions? Were there no other options?

It is very human to ask 'Why?' like this. Yet most scientists start in a much more modest way by asking *how* the solutions were arranged. Often that modesty has proved fruitful. In by-passing the 'Why?'s, science sometimes obtains answers it was never looking for. And so many 'Why?'s remain unanswered anyhow. Too frequent and irrelevant excursions in philosophy and religion in search of an answer to the question 'Why?' led many scientists to exclude the question by Occam's razor.[7] Others have endeavoured partial answers with an anthropic principle.[8] They say that the evolutionary routes amaze us only because we notice them at the end of a long causal chain to intelligence, culture and religion. By noting the facts we come across criteria that we need for our existence.

In my research and my thinking about justice, peace and the integrity of creation, the 'How?'s are more relevant than the 'Why?'s. The windows opened by the 'How?'s show many essentials of earth and life of which the 'Why?'s are not clear to us. Wonder about the pathways to intelligent life on a lonely and probable unique planet is important. Had the Psalmists known more amazing 'How?'s, they would again have made new songs to guide us on our rugged yet vulnerable planet. Wondering makes one more careful.

IV. Accident? Serendipity? Providence?

Did it all happen by accident? Concepts of accident and chance are firmly rooted in modern science, which has abandoned the determinism of previous centuries. For instance, unpredictable chaotic fluctuations make weather forecasts more than a week in advance nearly impossible, no matter what computational power is available. Physics can tell us with astounding accuracy how nature works, but the same physics teaches that its ultimate accuracy invariably ends up in a basic uncertainty.

Did it all happen by serendipity, serendipity which gives unexpected answers to questions we never asked? Penicillin was found by serendipity. More subtly than through Archimedes' 'Eureka', it dawned on Newton that his laws not only described *how* the planets moved, but also related to the question, never asked before, of why an apple falls to the ground. This serendipity from observing falling apples already shifts the 'How?' towards the 'Why?', but at the same time warns us that there may be more about which mortals on earth have no notion.

Did it all happen by providence? Those who wrestle with God always face the temptation to ask their 'Why?'s. But the faithful ones will not always expect ultimate rational answers. They are able to leave questions unanswered while at the same time anchoring their roots and ethics in biblical providence. Others without these roots will understand that the wondering provoked by the science touches on the essentials of religion. They can share with us and we with them a common cause for action on behalf of justice, peace and the integrity of creation.

V. Life through death

For those who want to see, God is a God of overwhelming dynamics and diversity, with creation and evolution taking place by the coming and going of stars, the coming and going of species, the coming and going of individuals. These dynamics brought about *homo sapiens*, us. 'Life through death' is a message of science as well as of the Bible.

Individuals of all higher species, man included, die (there is still debate over bacteria and unicellular organisms). Why? It is conceivable that cells or organisms could renew themselves *ad infinitum*. But this never happens in nature. Trees seem to approach infinite renewal by making a new outer bark each year, while their inner core of wood is in principle not exposed to death. When protected against fires or diseases, the streams of sap from roots to leaves can continue age after age. But ultimately even the Methusalehs among the trees, the sequoias and the bristle cones, will die from old age. Sooner or later the individuals of all species die. Why? Almost irresistibly, human beings of all times have wondered why the good God whom they seek allows death. Again, instead of giving a direct answer it is helpful to make an indirect statement: from the way in which God developed life, the 'how', we can perceive that God could not prevent death if there were to be life at all. God does not like death, but God needed death as an instrument for creating life.

'Life at the expense of other life, the survival of the fittest' may agree neither with justice, peace and the integrity of creation nor with the Christian faith, but it leaves us with insoluble issues in ecology between science and theology. Many species, our own not excluded, evolved by mechanisms with embarrassing cruelty. 'If God watches the sparrow fall,' wrote McDaniel, 'then he does so from a great distance.'[9] He is writing about pelicans, and how these stately birds usually lay two eggs, the second two days after the first. Because the energy balance of most pelicans allows them to raise only one young, the chick hatched earlier drives the later one out of the nest. Nine times out of ten the latter dies of abuse and starvation. The parent pelicans cannot waste precious parental energy on it. Cruel though this mode of parenting is, from an evolutionary perspective it has survival value to pelicans. The second chick is from a 'back-up egg': an insurance policy in case of accident or the imperfection of the first one. Neither the parents nor the older chick should be condemned, since they are both genetically conditioned to act as they do. The treatment of the hapless chick is a sub-routine in a larger evolutionary process. McDaniel put it very well: God is not indictable for this suffering; God does not like it, but could not and cannot prevent this process if there was to be life at all. Divine power knows limits and constraints. God is not all-powerful: God does not like death or suffering, but evidently could not avoid it.

In nature we often encounter things to embarrass us. Bird-watchers quickly learn to keep an emotional distance from insoluble issues. The goshawk, a magnificent hunter, catches what it can to feed its young. Its prey can be the baby tit, which then never returns to its nest again. And the drama leaves us at a loss where to place our sympathy: with the young hawks or with the baby tits in our garden. Yet hawk and tit are millions of years older than the human race, and evidently possess excellent survival values.

VI. Co-operating with God

Human beings are younger than most species around them: they developed fast and in a unique way as the only creature with the intellectual and moral capacity to act politically, ecologically and religiously. Moreover, human beings are the only creatures which can add non-anthropocentric components to their acts. With these attributes, they are predestined to a vocation of co-operating with God. They can start this vocation by taking to heart all that lives, and by educating themselves and their offspring to respect ecological limits set by a covenant. Always in combat with their counterparts, those bent on diabolical destruction, they may not acquiesce in the mass extinction and destruction of creation.

'We want to live together with all life that wants to live.' It is hardly conceivable that Dr Schweitzer or anyone else in his time could have foreseen the implications of his words. We are now slowly starting to recognize them: sharing our planet with all that lives restricts the pattern of our life and our use of land, air, water and biomass. The planet harbours large numbers of specific species with specific habitats, some of them in the rain forests and deep seas hardly studied. With growing ecological insight, human beings have to respect these habitats. This implies that we have to reserve and protect a large number of varied landscapes for nature, when possible achieving broad public acceptance: justice, peace and the integrity of creation needs to find a place within the hearts of all human beings.

For the twenty per cent of species which will have disappeared by the end of this century our concern comes too late. But it must not be too late to prevent an even higher percentage disappearing in the next century. This twenty per cent already calls for the immediate concern of religious, scientific and political organizations with existing global networks. Now that in the 1990s the angels from heaven have brought human beings a breathing space for demilitarization, one suggestion arises automatically: see peace in a non-anthropocentric sense by reformulating 'military defence of human beings' as 'defence of life', with a diligent reallocation of military funding for defending species. Much may be possible without guns and war, but with investments of one or two tenths of the present military budget and manpower. 'Now is the time.'[10]

VII. A finite earth

Justice, peace and the integrity of creation can be formulated with alternative words and complementary accents. For instance, by saying: *not at the expense of future generations; not at the expense of the Third World; not with the extinction of species*. Making any of these phrases specific inexorably leads to the problems we cause by our energy consumption, resulting in – among other things – more greenhouse emissions than can be absorbed by the finite atmosphere. The concentration of the severest greenhouse gas CO_2 increases rapidity; without JPIC, humankind will cause a doubling of CO_2 by about thirty-five years from now. Contrary to some press stories, there is reasonable agreement among experts that CO_2 doubling implies global warming. By how much is still uncertain, but the most likely rise in temperature after a doubling of greenhouse gases has now been narrowed down to 2° or 3° Celsius: 2° will be serious for the North and near catastrophic for the South; 3° implies sheer global catastrophe. Whereas cynics remark that the Baltic sea will become the Riviera of the twenty-first century, thought guided by JPIC turns with horror to the death and destruction to be expected in tropical and sub-tropical areas. There are uncertainties, but it is clear that the greenhouse gases 1. increase rapidly; 2. are caused by human beings; and 3. come largely from the North.[11] The warming means 4. formations of deserts and famine in the South; 5. the flooding of densely populated coastal areas; and 6. the destruction of habitat and ongoing extinction every-where.

A stabilization of the atmosphere requires a rigid ceiling for CO_2 and other greenhouse gases. But a global CO_2 ceiling at what level? At 0.030% near the pre-industrial level? Or at the 1990 status quo of 0.036%? Or at the CO_2 doubling value of 0.054%? Reflection on this may have far-reaching consequences. Failure to reflect on it would be worse – and lead to catastrophe. A healthy biosphere imposes constraints on human consumption *and* human numbers. The product of the average use of energy per person and the number of persons determines the world's energy use. In 1990 this amounted to 2.6 kilowatts times 5.3 billion persons, or in total 14 terawatts.[12] Both the per-person consumption and the size of the population show a clear tendency to increase,[13] and they have still to be related to the extinction of species.

By extending limits, humankind has known times of flourishing. With improved hunting methods, Cro-Magnon man became master of the Eurasian continent; the first agriculture and husbandry allowed culture and towns; law and organization allowed a Roman empire; after Columbus two new and almost empty continents offered new land: first an industrial, then a green and now a gene revolution offer new food supplies, albeit with cheap fossil energy.

By overstepping limits humankind has also known times of distress and starvation. After excessive pressure from hunting the large game disappeared; deforestation and erosion followed over-grazing and exhaustion of the land; wrong technology led to collapse; and each technological achievement was followed by over-population. In our day the green and the gene revolutions also demand their prices: debatable infrastructures and rapid consumption of finite energy reserves for cheap fertilizer – and last but not least, extinction of species.

With others, I conclude that while we have widened some limits in a positive sense, we have overstepped others to an immense degree in a negative sense. Respect for species and for the rights of later generations calls for restraint: for a lower global use of energy and for a reduction in the world's population. Compared to what we thought a quarter of a century ago, our situation is more serious than ever.

1. Twenty-five years ago, few were aware that at the end of this century twenty per cent of species will be extinct. This percentage is a sign of the degree to which we have overstepped limits, and the acute threat of a larger percentage in the next century would represent an even greater degree of overstepping.

2. Twenty-five years ago, the green revolution and later the gene revolution were seen exclusively as blessings. We now learn that they require unrealistic cheap energy and doubtful infrastructures.

3. Twenty-five years ago, people though of 'new' land without taking into account the destruction of habitat for flora and fauna.

4. Twenty-five years ago, the Club of Rome reported on the limits to growth. Who mis-labelled their report 'pessimistic'? It was written before there was a hole in the ozone layer and the greenhouse effect.

5. If twenty-five years ago we were worried about a world population of 10 billion or larger, now we have to worry about a further 5 billion or more. We need to talk not only of stabilization but also of reduction.

VIII. Consumption, population and extinction

Justice, peace and the integrity of creation are interrelated. Similarly, population, consumption and respect for species (or their negatives: overpopulation, overconsumption and extinction) are interrelated, too. Public attention often singles out just one of these three. Consumers agree that overpopulation is the world's main problem: there are too many poor people, and with cognitive dissonance these consumers point a finger to the South. However, from the perspective of JPIC we might counter that consumption is the world's main problem. There are too many rich people, and one baby in the industrialized world will pollute the earth ten to a hundred times more than a baby born in the developing world. Here a finger points to the North. And neither of the two perspectives has yet taken into account the disappearance of species. Figure 1 brings over-population, overconsumption and extinction together; each is of seemingly

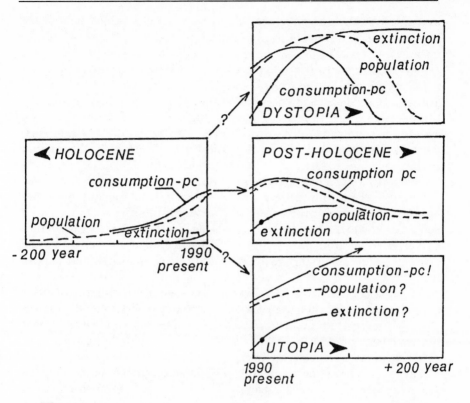

Figure 1

Population, consumption (per capita = pc) and extinction in two hundred years, past (left) and future (the three scenarios on the right). Until the 1950s the extinction is still hardly visible, but then it rises steeply to reach 20% at the end of the century. Many people expected, at least until recently, a utopia with ever-growing consumption in the hope of population stabilization (how?), and ignoring extinction. Utopia is unrealistic dreamland; dystopia is not unrealistic unless human behaviour changes; the violation of ecological limits end in collapse. A realistic post-Holocene period with sustainable and participatory human societies will require a fighting spirit.

Approximate vertical scales for the three curves are as follows: up to a population of 12 billion; up to 5 kilowatts per capita of commercial energy; and up to 100% for extinction as a cumulative percentage of what was alive at the left side of the diagram only two centuries ago.

insoluble complexity. Together they form a task for which no solitary human being, however willing to co-operate with God, will possess a ready-made set of answers.

The diagram on the left of figure 1 shows the steady increase of the three parameters in the last 200 years. They form the last two centuries of the geological period called Holocene. It is beyond question that humankind is bringing this period to a close: in our lifetime, for better or worse. Are we entering a dreamland utopia with ever-growing consumption? Or a doomed dystopia after reaching the point of 'finished is finished'? Or can humankind muster its unique capacities to fight for a realistic post-Holocene period as a tomorrow to which our children can look forward with eager expectation?

Utopia with lasting material growth is dreamland: unattainable no matter how temptingly it is proclaimed by short-term thinkers with misplaced authority, and to the despair of those who dare to think about justice within the wider 200-year horizon of fig. 1. We live on a finite planet with finite possibilities for material growth and with finite resistance to mismanagement.

Dystopia is undeniably the abyss on the edge of which humankind is teetering. When lawyers and politicians see no new way to global regulations, when captains of industry want no constraints, when few care about the death of nature, then we are *en route* to dystopia, with the destruction of creation, collapse and starvation.

The aim of justice, peace and the integrity of creation is a realistic post-Holocene period, whatever changes may be needed for such a future. Written history tells us that prophets and spiritual counsellors often perform poorly when meddling in short-term politics. We shall not over-rate their capacities here. But written history tells us about real catastrophes when kings and presidents are deaf to spiritual guidance for the longer term. The Creator must have foreseen the fate of a creation running out of hand in which by the mixed blessings of technology the human race will quickly exhaust its resources and by the mixed blessings of medicare populations will suddenly grow beyond the earth's capacity to sustain them. Was it with a view to this that humankind received knowledge and insight about the good and evil of 1990s technology? In order to be able to co-operate with God?

IX. Final remarks

It is now becoming clear that humankind has reached ecological limits in society and politics, though this realization is late and is mostly in anthropocentric terms. Opinion polls confirm a growing willingness to reduce levels of consumption in order to protect the environment, provided that the reduction is shared by everyone. This proviso points to the need for general regulations: global law. How can one own the atmosphere? How can it be that a few overload the atmosphere at the cost of bringing death and extinction elsewhere?

The thousand things to readjust have not yet all been listed, and not all the right words are yet in the right places. By and large, so far we have yet to achieve a consistent ethic. But we do see boundaries which we want to respect: technology may not remain normative. That which is 'possible' is not always 'allowed'; potentiality is not always permission. The urgent need for action hardly allows time to wait for global regulation. There must be women and men willing to start now, today, a life-style in keeping with JPIC: recognizable, realistic, practicable and future-orientated, *en route* for an acceptable post-Holocene age.

We must attempt this by:

reducing our private consumption to a cyclical economy, recognizable by a yearly specification of our energy usage.

standing up for non-anthropocentric components in all world religions, with:

global ceilings to greenhouse emissions;

cultural communication without excessive travelling and streams of paper;

advanced JPIC studies at one or more world universities.

Can the JPIC movement be instrumental in offering guidance and a home to a group prepared to live out JPIC?

On a cosmological scale, sun and earth are not yet old. In that respect we are living in the morning rather than the evening of the cosmos. Human beings have no right to cause a dystopia within a time-span of 200 years. We cannot be better than God. But perhaps God made our history on a little planet in a large universe open-ended and dependent on our actions in our time with awakening knowledge, insight and culture, calling us not to act destructively, in a pact with the devil, but to co-operate with God.

Notes

1. Psalm 139; Deut. 30.11f.; Gen.9.8f.; Job 28; Rom. 8.18f.
2. See *The Brundland Report. Our Common Future*, London 1987.
3. 'Energy for Planet Earth', *Scientific American*, September 1990.
4. Pope John Paul II, Celebration of the World Day of Peace, 1990.

5. Belgic Creed, article 2, on the living creatures, both small and great, being like letters in a beautiful book.

6. CO_2 at present forms 0.036% of the atmosphere. Anthropogenic CO_2 emission causes 50% of global warming, methane 16%, CFCs 14%, others 20%. Global emission for 1990 amounts to 5.6 billion tons of carbon, of which 24% comes from North America (5.1 tons per head), 19% from the USSR (3.5 tons) and 21% from Europe (2.4 tons).

7. Occam's razor is often applied in science to exclude from formal theory what cannot be experimentally verified.

8. The 'anthropic principle' gives human beings a central place in the cosmos. In its weak form it holds that intelligent life occurs only in a cosmos which satisfies boundary conditions which explain 'accidents' in evolution.

9. J. B. McDaniel, *Of God and Pelicans*, Louisville 1989.

10. World Council of Churches, *Now is the Time*, Seoul Final Document and Other Texts, 1990.

11. J. van Klinken, *Het Derde Punt*, Kampen 1989.

12. 1 terawatt $= 10^{12}$ watts: it is a measure for the usage of energy.

13. A ceiling of total energy use (e.g. 7 terawatts, or half of the present value) can still be achieved differently. The post-Holocene scenario of Fig. 1 sketches a mid-course in which the curves for consumption and population both end at one third of the vertical scale. The same ceiling is possible with a higher consumption by a smaller population (with a DINKI – double income and no kids – world as an extreme) and also with a larger population consuming less per head (with periodic starvation as an extreme).

Foundations and Perspective for an Ecological Ethics. The Problem of Responsibility for the Future as a Challenge to Theology

Werner Kroh

There is no argument over the increase of ecological problems in recent decades. The potential danger they pose calls for an ethical orientation, but it is not immediately clear what this orientation might be and what conviction is carried by normative statements about the degree and limits of the further industrial and scientific application of technology. Commands and prohibitions which are only tailored to specific problems do not go far enough, because their presuppositions are constantly overtaken by the rapid changes in our capacities. Moreover their criteria, which are related to the results of sometimes extremely complex technical and scientific research, easily lose sight of the overall problems of ecology. In addition, the public often has the impression that those who bear social responsibility (for example on ethical commissions in politics and industry) themselves have conflicts of interests and that other than ethical perspectives play a key role in decisions. For all these reasons, what is called for is a single concept, capable of being understood and tested, which covers the various individual ethical questions and opens up an overall perspective. In this article I shall describe Hans Jonas's approach, using an ethics of responsibility, and Karl-Otto Apel's approach, using an ethics of discourse. Both seek to meet the demands of such a concept. An investigation of them which is initially mutual and critical leads beyond both positions and covers those points of discussion which are central to a theological concern with the problems addressed: the concepts of subject and reason, the relationship between truth and history, and finally the problem of collective responsibility for the future and its institutionalization. But to begin with, let us recall the scenario to which ethical questioning must relate.

I. Problems common to ecology and ethics

The so-called politics of *détente* and the social changes in Eastern Europe have lessened fears of an atomic war in Europe. At the same time, as a result of the catastrophe at the nuclear power station at Chernobyl and regular technical defects in many installations which produce nuclear energy and process or store atomic fuels, politicians have come under increasing pressure to develop alternative sources of energy with much greater vigour and so initiate a departure from nuclear power. Certainly as a result of this, questions of the military and non-military use of nuclear energy, which some years ago were still also at the centre of ecological discussion, have faded into the background. That does not mean that they have become in any way irrelevant from an ethical perspective, but they are possibly open to a more sober and unprejudiced treatment. On the other hand (in autumn 1990), the dangers of a war with biological and chemical weapons, which for a long time had been put out of mind, are again being increasingly discussed as a result of the Gulf crisis. Along with the 'new' ecological problems, the novelty of which consists predominantly in their dramatic intensification and global extension, in the present complex of problems an ambivalent overall situation is being expressed. There are feelings of helplessness in the face of the overwhelming mass of possible dangers, and at the same time the awareness of a new dimension of responsibility: the knowledge that there is an intrinsic connection between the creation of world-wide justice, the achievement and safeguarding of peace, and the preservation of creation. Partisan interests and concerns continue to be implemented unchanged, but there is an insight that the world is more than the human environment, and that the preservation of the world is inseparably connected with the fate of humankind. All this should remind us that questions of an ecological ethic should not be approached too narrowly, if the solutions are to be viable. What is being sought is an ethics of responsibility for the future, which will first provide the framework for the appropriate treatment of the specific problems of ecology and the possibilities of solving them. The foundations and perspectives for such an ethic are the subject of this article and of the positions which are discussed in it.

In a critical discussion with Hans Jonas[1], Karl Otto Apel states that the task of philosophical ethics now lies less in proposing material norms related to the situation 'than in the analysis of the normative conditions of the organization of collective responsibility on the various possible levels of practical discourse'.[2] Nowadays, he argues, it is virtually impossible to deduce material norms from general principles which all those involved in the argument necessarily recognize – like, for example, the fundamental principle of collective responsibility. On the other hand, only a differentiation and mediation between scientific, technical, strategic and ethical rationality could make an effective impact on the present crisis and protect both ethics and society from well-meaning but ultimately naive and irrational reactions which are short cuts.[3] In pursuing this basic assumption Apel describes an ethic of discourse, in comparison with an ethic of responsibility as argued for by Jonas, as a two-stage ethic: first a renewed transcendental philosophy is to provide the basis for the fundamental principle of collective responsibility; then the principle of discourse in organizing collective responsibility is to be used for grounding any new material norms that are to be formulated in relation to the situation. He accepts Jonas's view that the necessity of such a foundation must grow out of the relationship between actual facts (which we also create anew on each occasion) and human ability: technological and political power.[4]

In what follows I shall now attempt to work out the foundation and basic concern of an ecological ethics on the basis of Hans Jonas's 'principle of responsibility', connect this with the ethics of discourse, and formulate questions to both positions from which a genuine theological approach to an ecological ethic can be recognized. In this process it will also become clear that the task of theology cannot either consist in a mere duplication of already existing ethical theories or norms, or be exhausted in well-meant but rationally inadequate moral appeals for justice, peace and the integrity of creation.

II. Responsibility for the future in the face of ecological problems of the present

Since the publication of the first study by the Club of Rome on *The Limits of Growth* in 1972, not only have the number and extent of ecological problems increased, but also their 'quality' and their potential danger for the future of the earth and of humankind. This increase can already be read from the 1980 US Presidential Report *Global 2000*, and may have progressed further since then. If initially the population explosion, world food supplies and the scarcity of resources stood in the foreground, in the meantime the range of problems has been extended and intensified: the warming of the earth's atmosphere, the enlargement in the hole in the ozone layer and the cutting down of the rain forests are leading to an increase in the surface areas of the oceans and a decrease in summer rain; in the form of the so-called greenhouse effect this affects the stability of vegetation and agricultural production, and thus ultimately works back to the food supply for the population of the world and the exploitation of the limited natural sources of energy. And all this is overlaid by an exponential growth in population which reduces the possibilities of influencing the effects of this development by means of medical and hygenic measures and the success of efforts at education, while intensifying the increasing ecological dangers to crisis level and raising the possibility of military conflicts, especially since, on these presuppositions, the struggles over the distribution of the scanty goods and resources will increase further.

Extending the horizon of responsibility

Along with the fact that human beings have themselves become the object of technology, Jonas sees as the fundamentally new element in the present world situation which is to be met by an 'ethic of responsibility for the future' (175) the presence of these dangers which were only conjured up by the possibilities of modern technology. For the new element relates equally both to the facts created by human beings and to the ethical action that is called for: 'The subjection of nature with the aim of providing human happiness' has itself become the greatest challenge to human existence, and the 'new territory of collective praxis that we have entered with high technology is still a no man's land for ethical theory' (7). Moreover, in the question of human responsibility, all previous ethics, including ethics for the future, could begin from a sphere of human action which in principle was limited: at all events, only the immediate consequences for the next generation(s) were of significance to ethics. 'No former ethics had to take into account the global conditions of human life and the distant future, indeed the very existence of the species' (28). Finally, the present is also different from all former situations by virtue of its dynamic and – in epistemological terms – paradoxical character. For on the one hand we know more than former generations (at the level of analytical-causal knowledge and its technological and instrumental application); on the other hand we know less, because we live in a period of constitutional change, which means 'that we have to reckon with constantly new things, without being able to work them out; we know that change is certain, but not what this change will lead to (216f.). According to Jonas, if the basis for a new ethic is not to fall short, it must extend into metaphysics, 'which alone asks the question why people should be in the world at all, in other words why the unconditional imperative holds, to guarantee their existence for the future' (8). In this connection he accuses the Hellenistic-Jewish-Christian ethic in particular of a 'heedless anthropocentrism' (95), to which the principle of 'duty to human beings' which he advocates does not succumb, because when it comes to the alternative, 'preservation or destruction', the interest of humankind coincides with that of the rest of life and through the extended power of human beings also extends to their responsibility for the biosphere (245, 248).

Following on from Kant's categorical imperative, Jonas makes the statement (initially as an axiom, without offering any justification): 'Act in such a way that the effects of your actions are compatible with the permanence of authentic human life on earth'; or, negatively, 'Act in such a way that the effects of your action are not destructive towards the future possibility of such life'; or, simply, 'Do not endanger the conditions for an indefinite continuation of humankind on earth', or, again put positively: 'Include in your present choice the future integrity of human beings as an object of your will' (36). Jonas is aware that it is difficult, and perhaps even impossible, to justify this obligation not to put the existence of future generations at risk in the interest of the present generation, properly understood, without bringing in religion (36).[5] But since both the Christian ethic of a fulfilment in a future world and the Marxist politics of utopia have failed, an attempt must be made to create an ethic for the future which is non-eschatological and in some sense anti-utopian (46). Characteristic of this is a 'heuristics of fear' (8): in the face of progress it stresses the need for preservation and gives priority to the possible disaster that modern technology can bring over its more hopeful aspects (it differs, of course, from mere fantasies of fear). For the acceleration of developments fed by technology leaves less and less time and freedom of movement for self-corrections (72).

Do we optimize life or annihilate it?

In the last resort, the possibilities of modern technology open up two extreme perspectives: the over-confident expectation of further improving the conditions in which human beings live in the direction of attaining the supreme good, or – as the supreme evil – the self-destruction of humankind and the earth. Balancing out the two possibilities suggests the priority of the second. 'For one can live without the supreme good but not with the supreme evil . . . Now this proviso – namely that the greatest evil can only be warded off and the greatest good cannot be introduced, which in some circumstances can justify total commitment to the interests of others in their interest – does not legitimate the great ventures of technology' (79). There is an 'unconditional obligation on human beings of existence' (80), which in the case of decisions gives priority to prognoses of disaster over prognoses of salvation. It is expressed in the ethical principle: 'Human existence or human nature as a whole may never be made the stake in the wagers of action' (81). But how can the 'unconditional duty of humankind to exist' itself be given a further foundation?

Here further considerations lead into the sphere of metaphysics. According to Jonas, it is part of the ontological idea of human beings that their existence *should* be (91). A decision about the existence of humankind in itself is less a decision about the *right* of future generations than about their *duty*, 'namely their duty to true humanity, in other words their capacity to do this duty, the capacity to talk to one another at all, of which we could perhaps rob them with the alchemy of our "utopian" technology. It is *our* basic duty to watch over this in the face of the future of humankind from which all duties towards future human beings are first derived' (89).[6] The mark of human beings, that they are the only ones who can have responsibility, at the same time means that they *must* have it for others of their kind (185). Whatever judgment is to be passed on the previous history of humankind, and whatever answer is to be given to the question whether it is worth continuing, 'It is the self-binding, ever-transcendent possibility which must be held open through existence. Precisely the preservation of this possibility as a cosmic responsibility represents the duty to exist' (186).

But even if we suppose that human beings also perceive the greatest possible extent of their responsibility for the future (and we shall return to this in the next part), the decisive question is how nature relates to the intensified technological and economic attack. 'So in the last resort the question is not how much human beings will still be in a position to do . . . but how much of this nature can bear' (329). There are 'limits to the toleration of nature' which in respect of basic problems (the provision of food, the limited reserves of raw material, questions of energy conservation and the problem of global warming) are already recognizable, even if they cannot be established exactly. Here the insights of biologists, agronomists, chemists, climatologists, economists, engineers, etc, must be combined in a 'global environmental science' (330), on the results of which any ethic of future responsibility depends. For all the uncertainty of forecasting and extrapolation, however, it should be clear that only with a 'veto against utopia' (337), i.e. an abandonment of increases in global production and aggressive technology, is there still a possibility of preventing the annihilation of nature by human beings and thus the self-destruction of the human race. And it was precisely the avoidance of this double effect which was aimed at with the principle of responsibility.

III. The organization of collective responsibility by means of the principle of discourse

The expert knowledge of yesterday has largely become the collective consciousness of the present. Similarly, present-day extended expert knowledge about the state of the earth and the ecological dangers which we must expect if we continue our present treatment of the earth and of humankind must be introduced into a collective awareness of the future. Running counter to this is the legitimate assumption that the gulf between knowledge and action has never been so great as it is today, and is continuing to increase. There is therefore a great and more urgent need than ever for the organization of collective responsibility in politics, society and culture, so as to get to grips with the damage that has already been done and to avert the dangers which threaten.

Those who bear responsibility for the future
In considering the question how this collective responsibility is to be organized for the future, Jonas now ends up in a basic dilemma. On the one hand he is aware that the limitation of power 'must start from society, since no private insight, responsibility or anxiety is equal to the task' (254), and 'only a high degree of social discipline imposed by politics can see that advantages in the present are subordinated to long-term requirements of the future' (255). Indeed the issue is no longer simply one of moderation in the use of power but of moderation in its acquisition.[7] On the other hand, Jonas believes that the *new* power which is called for (at a tertiary level), which not only protects human beings from themselves but also protects nature from human beings (253f.), can only be acquired technically and intellectually by an élite (263); consequently, 'in the coming harshness of a policy of responsible denial, democracy (in which those with interests in the present have the most prominent say) is useless, at least for the moment'. And for the moment, even though it may be 'repugnant', the only possible choice is 'between different forms of "tyranny"' (269).

At this point Jonas's argument meets up with, and at the same time fundamentally differs from, the approach of an ethics of discourse in respect of the question who is responsible for the future, as this is raised in the introductory quotation from Karl-Otto Apel. Certainly he, too, begins from the dilemma that whereas nowadays the need for an ethic which entails an intersubjective commitment, an ethic of responsibility in solidarity, is more urgent than ever before, the rational foundation for such an ethic has never been as difficult as it is in the present.[8] Apel, however, looks for the solution only from 'an application to history of the ethic of communication as an ethic of responsibility'.[9] In the context of this solution, Jonas' élite, in the form of the community in which communication is really achieved, is only a transitional phenomenon on the way towards the ideal communicative community which is ultimately envisaged, and recourse to any form of 'tyranny' in this connection is quite unacceptable. For even in the case of a real communicative community there is a need for a responsibility in solidarity for the solving of problems, equal rights for all in the solving of problems, and the principle that 'all valid solutions to problems – particularly those which are ethically relevant – would have to be capable of achieving a consensus of all the members of the unlimited, ideal communicative community, if they could be discussed together'.[10] In addition to the responsibility of solidarity which has already been mentioned, the characteristics of the ideal communicative community, which is already anticipated in the real community, even if the facts tell against it, are equal rights and the capacity for consensus along with the removal of all asymmetries (including social assymetries), freedom from pressure, a transparency and lack of distortion in argument, and the readiness of every participant in discourse to justify the conceptions introduced into the discourse and to be open to reasoned refutation.[11]

However, for Apel, too, this raises the question how these conditions can be institutionalized in a concrete historical situation which is always already shaped by conflicts of interest, and are compatible with decisions of conscience which also necessarily have to be made under the pressure of time.[12] We shall return to that in due course. First of all, two further objections to Jonas' conception arising from the ethics of discourse must be discussed. They also help towards further clarification of the approach of the ethics of discourse to our theme.

Conservation or progress?

Jonas begins from the thesis that the idea of progress and the utopia implied in it gets involved in an irresolvable conflict with the idea of the conservation of nature and consequently argues that it is necessary first of all to construct 'an ethics of conservation, of protection, of prevention, and not of progress and perfection' (249). Against this, Apel asks whether, specifically on the presupposition – which he shares – that in the present situation it is important to rescue the existence, survival and dignity of human beings, these 'can be rescued by merely preserving the present situation. More precisely, is not the nature of human beings and their environment, long since transformed by technology and social culture, such that they cannot be preserved without a regulative idea of technological and social progress? Is not the possibility of an ethical preservation of human dignity, in particular, *a priori* linked to the condition that it must always first be realized – specifically as a world-wide restoration of social conditions which represent human dignity?'[13] To this degree the task of realizing an ideal communicative community also includes 'the abolition of the class society, or, to put this in terms of communication theory: the removal of all socially-conditioned assymetries in interpersonal dialogue'.[14]

The slogan 'conservation or progress' poses a false alternative, which must be resolved in the sense of 'conservation also through progress': 'The strategy for survival takes on its meaning through a long-term strategy of emancipation.'[15] Moreover, the recognition that in theory all potential partners in discourse have equal rights (as a presupposition of any serious argument and at the same time as an anticipation, in the face of the facts, of the ideal communicative community which is to be realized progressively), and that all valid solutions also need to be coherent and command a consensus, implies 'that the communicative community of humanity which now exists will continue in the future under conditions of equal rights'.[16] In connection with the former, Apel speaks of two fundamental regulative principles for anyone's long-term strategy: 'All activity must be concerned, first, with guaranteeing the survival of the human species as the real communicative society and, secondly, with bringing about the ideal communicative society in the real one.'[17] The ultimate justification for the ethics of discourse thus achieves two things: it contains – as in Jonas – a rational reason why there should also be a human species in the future, and it answers – in a different sense from Jonas – the question 'whether it is possible to advocate an ethic of the conservation of existence and human dignity without at the same time advocating an ethics of progress in the realization of human dignity'.[18]

Two conceptions of responsibility

The second objection relates to Jonas's claim about the 'discontinuance of reciprocity in the ethics of the future' (84ff.). What is meant here is the idea of the reciprocity of rights (of one individual) and duties (of the other) which normally correspond; however, this is an idea which fails when applied to the problem of responsibility. Since that which does not exist cannot make any claims, its rights cannot be violated either. Nevertheless, the ethics of a responsibility for the future asserts that the present generation has duties towards those to come. Whereas for Jonas the justification and indeed the necessity of this (one-sided) obligation is grounded in ontological responsibility for the idea of the human being, Apel doubts whether the question of responsibility is about a discontinuance of reciprocity at all. For, 'Jonas's model instances, i.e. the responsibility of parents for children and the responsibility of the statesman for the weal and woe of the citizens entrusted to him, do not in my view show that responsibility is a relationship of reciprocity. They show, rather, that the main responsibility of human beings for one another is a potential relationship, which becomes actual only according to the criteria of a *de facto* progress in power.' [19] And precisely such responsibility in solidarity is what the communicative society seeks to bring about. To this degree Jonas's principle 'You should since you can' applies. However, the specific duties of the individual and the socially binding norms emerge only in the discourse of those involved, about what consequences and side-effects are to be expected if the norms proposed are followed. Moreover, the norms derive their binding character and legitimability from a principle which lies deeper, according to which we are generally obliged to take responsibility. And to the degree that we 'have always already recognized this "should" in freedom as rational beings', [20] Kant's statement, 'You can, for you should', also remains valid. For Apel this also resolves this alternative of Jonas's along the lines of a complementary relationship.

Let us now once again take up the question of what consequences the foundations for an ethic of responsibility for the future which have been developed so far have in terms of their being given institutional form. Here we are talking about problems which are common to the two approaches discussed here. At the same time they lead beyond these positions, and therefore form a starting point for some concluding reflections on theological aspects of the foundations and perspectives of an ecological ethic.

IV. Questions and objections: Theological aspects of an ethic of responsibility for the future

The complementarity hitherto of apparently value-free scientific objectivity and the moral decision of the individual has proved unsatisfactory on both sides. First of all, the approach of an ethics of discourse seeks to make it clear that any rational argumentation and thus also the 'objectivity' of supposedly value-free science presupposes the validity of universal ethical norms. In particular this applies to the humane sciences, which are concerned with 'an understanding reconstruction of human actions, works and institutions, in short, with the self-understanding of human praxis in terms of its history'.[21] Finally, the instrumental and strategic transposition of scientific knowledge presupposes decisions about the goals of human praxis, but (*pace* Apel) these only in part have rational foundations and are predominantly derived from convictions of faith and also from irrational attitudes to life practised on the basis of long custom. Secondly, particularly in connection with the decision of the individual conscience, the question arises whether self-discipline is the only alternative to the 'spectre of tyranny' and whether the need for tyranny can be avoided only 'by taking ourselves in hand and again becoming stricter with ourselves'.[22] In other words, according to what criteria can the various decisions of conscience on the part of individuals be harmonized? And does the formation of a common will also lead to binding decisions (beyond conventions), so that responsibility for social practice based on solidarity is really possible?

The limitations of an ethics of discourse

Much as the concern for a post-conventional morality, an ethic of communication and formation of a democratic will are to be supported,[23] they do not lead out of a dilemma: rational grounds can be the decisive motives for action, but they need not be, and they are certainly not the only ones. But this difference does not just apply this side of the ideal communicative community, as Apel seems to suggest; at least, it cannot be shown that grounds and motives simply coincide in such a community. Even someone who is ready 'to make all human needs – as virtual claims – the concern of the communicative community',[24] need not yet be convinced that they can be harmonized through argumentation. Far less can this requirement guarantee action to match. The person who has been 'through-rationalized' in this sense evidently remains a fiction, even for Apel: even the obligation to collaborate in the 'approximative removal' of the difference between the real and the ideal communicative community cannot do away with what is in principle its character.[25] In addition, Apel could at least have taken into account the fact that outside institutionalized communication decisions of conscience also have to be made under pressure of time and that the importance of the tragic in human boundary situations may not be underestimated.[26] The more banal but nevertheless widespread obstacle in the way of a universal ethic of communication lies in the differences between basis and motive, insight and action, the community of discourse and the community of action. That human beings put their short-term interests above their long-term interests; that they subordinate the demands of the common good, which on the whole are also to their own advantage, to selfish ends; that in fact they do what they really do not want to do – all this must be taken seriously from an ethical perspective as an expression of freedom – in theological terms, as the human capacity for guilt – if it cannot be resolved in discourse.

One problem for the ethics of communication lies in the overcoming of the difference between theoretical and practical discourse. A basic ethical norm which obliges everyone also to observe binding agreements in practice[27] comes up against its external limits at precisely this point: rational reasons can be given for its validity, but it is impossible to require that it should be followed without giving up the presuppositions of communication theory. Jürgen Habermas also sees this limit when he states that it is by no means a matter of course that 'rules which are unavoidable within discourses can also claim validity outside arguments', and that the requirement for conditions of discourse with a normative content cannot be transferred from discourse to action.[28] Habermas speaks of forfeiting concrete morality, of which because of cognitive prejudice any universalistic morality must first take account, and through it make good corresponding forms of life it in order to be effective in practice.[29]

Two questions arise directly from this. Does not a communicative ethic thus presuppose not only the embedding of theoretical discourse in practical discourse but above all the embedding of communicative communities in living communities, so that potential claims are not only recognized but also realized, and ethical basic norms are not only looked at rationally but also have their validity observed in practice? But such living communities need more comprehensive motivations and traditions and a more supportive institutional form if they are to be capable of existing in the long term, and of providing communities of discourse. So we need to be ask whether the attempt to provide a 'rational' basis for basic ethical norms does not come to grief on an inner limit which is expressed precisely in this understanding of rationality which suddenly becomes visible in Apel when he talks about the function of the metaphysical (and also metaethical or speculative theological!) way of presenting the problems: 'The "analogous" language of metaphysics is to some degree justified as long as a more adequate formulation of the problem has yet to be achieved successfully.'[30]

The significance of anamnetic reason for ethics
What we can recognize here is a reduced understanding of rationality and at the same time an 'idealistic' concept of the subject. Both are also echoed in Habermas's reflective question whether 'as Europeans we can seriously understand concepts like morality and ethics, person and individuality, freedom and emancipation . . . without appropriating the substance of salvation-historical thought with a Jewish Christian origin,'[31] and in so doing he is talking of both metaphysical *and* religious questions. Is the 'advance formulation of a problem' in every case identical with its logically stringent form, and can someone who participates in practical discourse be reduced to a 'subject of a rationally grounded argument'? While both definitions are also necessarily conditions of particular forms of discourse and a communicative society, they do not form sufficient conditions for the understanding of rationality and subject. Here it becomes clear to what degree the theological claim draws attention to dimensions which in two respects burst the limits of a communicative society and the discursive ethics that it aims at.

First, in the communicative society (whether real or ideal) the relationship between the question of truth and the democratic discursive principle remains open. On the one hand democracy is understood as a process for forming a common will and arriving at a decision, and on the other hand it means a more comprehensive form of life (in terms of the democratizing of all spheres of life, society, etc.). In both cases it includes the validity of the majority principle, and it is not clear how the problem of obligation to the truth is related to that. The grounding of basic ethical norms in discourse itself implies a claim to truth which would have to be mediated in discourse along with the democratic formation of a common will. But does that not produce a *coincidentia oppositorum* which is incapable of resolution? To put the matter pointedly: can the question of truth and the question of a majority be reconciled (at least in *every* case)?

Secondly, an ethic of responsibility for the future needs to make fruitful use of the insight that Christianity is primarily not a community of argumentation but a community of recollection and narrative. It is only recollection which protects the communicative society from an ahistorical concept of rationality and prevents concrete moral action from being dissolved into the process of evolution. Communicative reason is not just directed towards remembrance in order to be effective in the interest of human freedom. In Apel's view the 'evaluative characteristic' is part of the objective constitution of the humane sciences. To this degree it is not historical reconstruction but recollection of the sufferings of the past which makes it possible to understand human praxis, and which makes it possible for human beings to understand themselves from their history. So there can be enlightenment about the actual historical processes of enlightenment and their halvings, thus smoothing the way to a more comprehensive realization of freedom. For without specific recollection of suffering, the contradictions of the modern history of freedom cannot be grasped, nor is it possible to overcome them. Furthermore, communicative reason must understand itself as anamnetic reason if it is to be put into practice as an interest in freedom.[32] Only such reflection protects even communicative reason from destroying its subjective basis and makes it possible for this reason to understand itself as an expression of interest in human freedom and justice and as resistance to any form of injustice and unfreedom. And finally, in an age when human actions have a global effect, when there is any question of 'a mobilization of moral imagination in the direction of "love of neighbour" which is *prima facie* abstract', [33] this notion is not just derived from Christian faith but is particularly, even more, directed towards the power of recollection, in order to provide a future orientation for human action.

The principles of responsibility and discursive ethics each in their own way pick up the theme of this issue, *No Heaven without Earth*, in order to work out the foundations and perspectives of an ethic of responsibility for the future. But from where do we get the courage and the power for self-discipline (Jonas)? Where do we get the stamina to anticipate again and again, against the facts, the ideal communicative community in the real community (Apel)? Where do we get the criteria for neither making our notions of justice, freedom, peace and the integrity of creation too narrow nor abandoning them in the face of reality? It is not abstract appeals to the Jewish-Christian tradition, but concrete recollection of the sufferings of the past that have to be endured in the historical and social struggles for injustice, peace and freedom, and of the hopes that have emerged from this suffering, which point also to the reversal of this theme in the form of a statement of promise and hope, which has a historically determined time and a concrete social location: 'No earth without heaven!'

Translated by John Bowden

Notes

1. H. Jonas, *Das Prinzip Verantwortung. Versuch einer Ethik für die technologische Zivilisation*, Frankfurt 1979, quoted from the 1986 Suhrkamp edition. Page references are to this work.

2. K.-O. Apel, *Diskurs und Vertanwortung. Das Problem des Übergangs zur postkonventionellen Moral*, Frankfurt 1990, 212.

3. Ibid., 258 n. 8.

4. Ibid., 211f.

5. For the connection between the concept of God, metaphysics and ethics in Jonas cf. W. Oelmüller, 'Hans Jonas. Mythos – Gnosis – Prinzip Verantwortung', *Stimmen der Zeit* 106, 1988, 343–51.

6. A complete account would at this point have to pursue Jonas's arguments about the 'priority of being over nothingness', the rooting of metaphysics in his theory of values (cf. 97ff.), and the reversal of the statement, 'You can, for you should' (cf. 23off.). I shall not attempt that here.

7. Cf. H. Jonas, *Technik, Medizin und Ethik. Zur Praxis des Prinzips Verantwortung*, Frankfurt 1985, 70.

8. Cf. Apel, *Diskurs* (n.2), 16.

9. Ibid., 10.

10. Ibid., 202. For the foundation of discursive ethics cf. also K.-O. Apel, *Transformation der Philosophie*, Frankfurt 1973, Vol. 2, 358–435; J. Habermas, *Moralbewusstsein und kommunikatives Handeln*, Frankfurt 1983, 53–125.

11. For this combination see Abel, *Transformation* (n.10), 402 n.61; id., *Diskurs* (n.2), 20f.; Habermas, *Moralbewusstsein* (n.10), 97–9.

12. Cf. Apel, *Transformation* (n.10), 426f.

13. Cf. Apel, *Diskurs* (n.2), 184.

14. Cf. Apel, *Transformation* (n.10), 432.

15. Ibid.

16. Cf. Apel, *Diskurs* (n.2), 203.

17. Cf. Apel, *Transformation* (n.10), 431.

18. Cf. Apel, *Diskurs* (n.2), 203.

19. Ibid., 196f.

20. Ibid., 198.

21. Cf. Apel, *Transformation* (n.10), 380.

22. Thus Jonas, in H. Jonas and M. Dieth (eds.), *Was für morgen lebenswichtig ist. Unentdeckte Zukunftswerte*, Freiburg 1983, 31.

23. Cf. Apel, *Diskurs* (n.2), 365f.; id., *Transformation* (n.10), 426.

24. Apel, *Transformation* (n.10), 425.

25. Thus Apel in W. Kuhlmann (ed.), *Moralität und Sittlichkeit. Das Problem Hegels und die Diskursethik*, Frankfurt 1986, 247, 249f.

26. Ibid., 427f.

27. Cf. ibid., 375.

28. Habermas, *Moralbewusstsein* (n.10), 96, cf. 115f.

29. Cf. ibid., 119.

30. Apel, *Transformation* (n.10), 418.

31. J. Habermas, *Nachmetaphysisches Denken. Philosophische Aufsätze*, Frankfurt 1988, 23.

32. Cf. J. B. Metz, 'Anamnetische Vernunft. Anmerkungen eines Theologen zur Krise der Geisteswissenschaften', in A. Honneth et al. (eds.), *Zwischenbetrachtungen. Im Prozess der Aufklärung*, Frankfurt 1989, 733–8.

33. Apel, *Transformation* (n.10), 388.

'Ecological Wisdom' and the Tendency towards a Remythologization of Life

John Carmody

Let us deal with this important question in three stages, treating progressively of 'ecological wisdom', the tendency towards a re-mythologization of life, and implications for future Christian praxis.

I. 'Ecological wisdom'

Whether explicitly or implicitly, many writers dealing with ecology suggest that the natural world has a wisdom that human beings neglect at their peril. The ecological crisis – the pollution and so dysfunction of such natural systems as those of the air, the land, and the waters – is the main evidence for this suggestion. Through our modern technology, we human beings have intervened in the processes of the natural world so excessively and unwisely that we have wounded physical creation. In addition to the perils that polluted air, land, and water hold for human beings, they are signs that we are killing the physical basis for life itself. In myriad places, noxious smog, acid rain, toxic chemicals, the greenhouse effect, the depletion of the ozone layer, and other undesirable changes in the overall system of the planet earth tell us that we are living unwisely. The way of life, and by inference the set of values, that the industrialized nations have developed seem to be inimical to the laws by which creation runs. 'Ecological wisdom' is the message encoded in those laws of creation, as the breakdown of nature now spotlights them. For many who write and lecture on ecology, the first thing that human beings have to do, if they are to save our planet and species, is to listen to the wisdom of the earth.[1]

When one tries to listen to the wisdom of the earth, what is one likely to hear? First, one is likely to hear many specific complaints. Emissions from automobiles and factories are fouling the air. Toxic chemicals are leaking from their containers and poisoning the land or the streams where they were deposited. Human developers are destroying the habitats of many animals, creating a huge list of endangered species. The pollution of the skies and deforestation are heating up the globe and threatening to melt the polar ice caps. Deforestation is also hastening erosion, making vast areas unproductive. Many human beings are suffering from ailments of the lungs and the respiratory system. Many others are threatened with poisoning by lead, mercury and other lethal elements. The list of complaints goes on and on. The seas, the rivers, the lakes; the trees, the animals; the air of the cities and the land of traditional farming areas; the bodies of miners, industrial workers, and little children playing in city lots – item after item in the newspapers shouts or whispers that a given set of relations between human beings or animals and the natural environment has fallen out of harmony.

Second, the wisdom of the earth expresses itself in the larger dysfunctions that one can now observe in nature and the questions that such dysfunctions raise about our contemporary way of life in the developed countries. Questions of where human beings are going to find the natural energy to maintain their societies during the twenty-first century, where they are going to find sufficient food and materials for shelter, how they are going to integrate their growing populations with their natural resources, and even how they are going to achieve a just distribution of their wealth, dovetail with questions about the dangers of nuclear energy, the pollution caused by cattle, the contribution of chemical and electro-magnetic pollution to the incidence of cancer in human beings, and numerous other societal issues. The larger message from nature is therefore that our present way of life in the developed countries is incompatible with a healthy physical environment.

Before we consider the mythopoeia that sometimes surrounds this way of depicting ecological wisdom, let us nail down the conclusion of any honest listening to the protests of creation. The conclusion is that human beings are now the major determinants of the health or illness, the future vitality or mortality, of the planet earth. We are the crucial factor, and at present our impact is more lethal than benign. Through the tens of thousands of years when our technological power was relatively slight, we could regard nature as an open field where we could work and play as we wished. The resources of nature were so great, and our numbers and powers were so relatively small, that we could use the resources of nature without heeding wider or longer-range consequences. When we had fouled one habitat, we could simply pick up and move on. Our impact on the overall system of the oceans was so slight that we could dump our garbage, deposit our human waste, with no worry that we were threatening the total health of the seas. We could not overfish, and even when we overhunted certain areas, or farmed the soil to exhaustion, the scale of our damage remained something that nature as a whole could contain. We were not strong enough to create serious desertification, or erosion, or smog, or extermination of great numbers of species. We lived with the myth that the physical world was ours to exploit as we needed or saw fit. All of that has now changed.

The sober wisdom that many commentators now hear in the cries of a wounded nature is that our human species has become a growing threat to the survival of the planet. Indeed, our leading way of life, the industrialized prosperity that nations of the First World want to expand and nations of the Third World often want to imitate, is bearing down on nature, like an executioner with noose in hand. If we continue our present patterns, we will wound nature so badly that it will never recover. The worst such wounding, of course, would occur through nuclear warfare. But even if the nations manage to avert nuclear warfare and destroy their stockpiles of horrendous weapons, the ways that we now transport ourselves, feed ourselves, clothe ourselves, build and furnish our homes, and communicate, conspire toward the death of the physical environment. The chemicals that we have come to depend upon are poisoning the earth, and those chemicals are ingredient in the way of life now desired by most of the human population.

The other side of this ultimate message from the earth is that we must change to a global lifestyle, an agreed way of interacting with nature to gain food and shelter, money and culture, that is much less injurious, and so probably is much simpler, consuming much less. We need to give nature time to recover from nearly a century's worth of unheeding assault. We have to allow those systems that can recover, can cleanse themselves of our pollutants, the opportunity to do so. Otherwise, nature will only continue to sicken, soon becoming irreversibly moribund. We have to stop the production of noxious emissions, spills, discharges, erosions, and the like dramatically enough to let nature convalesce. Minor changes in the lifestyle of the industrialized nations will not be sufficient. The entire set of interactions with nature that modern industrialization and commerce have created must come under review. Taking as our criterion the impact that any significant part of our current lifestyle has on the pollution of nature, we must determine to change everything that creates a serious threat to nature's vitality. And we must also think in terms of an overall, more than piecemeal, change in our way of life, because our various negative impacts have systemic implications. Nature is a series of interlocking systems. That is what the word 'ecology' itself suggests. If we are murdering nature, we have to desist and reform with a systematic effectiveness that parallels the systematic abuses we have created. This is a very complicated and demanding business, much more radical than what most political leaders have been willing to entertain. Indeed, it calls for a new vision of how human beings ought to interact with nature and live together in the future. Naturally, so ultimate a question lends itself to mythopoeia, in both bad and good ways – which brings us to our second topic.

II. The tendency towards a remythologization of life

When they contemplate the ecological changes that the wisdom of the wounded planet suggests, sensitive observers can begin searching for better models of human interaction with the physical environment. They can recall that people of small-scale societies, recent or prehistoric, seem to have had friendlier relations with nature. Certainly, such people have feared the might of nature, compared to which they have often felt helpless. On the other hand, they have blessed the light of their eyes and the air they breathed, the sun that gave them warmth and the earth that gave them food. With or without romantic indulgence, observers following the line of reflection have wondered whether the key to the ecological crisis doesn't lie in the loss of intimacy with nature that modern, industrialized culture has created. Mediaeval peasants felt tied to the cycles of the earth in ways that contemporary urbanites cannot. We need not pass over all the dismal aspects of mediaeval peasant life to wonder whether there aren't lessons in the rootedness that such a culture assumed. The physical earth was people's home. It was 'mother earth', the foundation for the 'fatherland' or 'mother-land' that culture created. And so many peoples of older, smaller-scale societies interacted with the trees and birds, the animals and plants, of their habitat relatively gently. Even when they had to hunt and fish, clear land and farm it, they could sense a need to reverence their fellow creatures. The earth was a living whole. Human beings were only one species, and not necessarily the most important one. That was the way that traditional American Indians, Africans, Asians, and even Europeans could feel.

Such a feeling tended to be fraught with perceptions of sacredness. The mysteries of life and death were patent enough, stark enough, to force people to wonder deeply about where they came from and where they were going, why life was sometimes so beautiful and sometimes so cruel. The famous paintings on the walls of ancient caves in France and Spain suggest people mesmerized by the wonder of both animal and human life. Fertility, the main protection against death, was an obvious preoccupation. When we come to peoples whose cultures we know better, we often find that myths of creation are the linch-pin. How the world was born is the basic pattern that all subsequent human creatures follow – building a village, raising a new house, celebrating the new year. The mythic mentality of such ancient peoples schooled them to think that the world is a living whole. Individual species are more consubstantial with one another than distinct. All plants and animals, even all rocks and streams, participate in the wonder of existence. All are alive, in some way, and all have rights. Naturally, human beings often trampled on these rights, as they often slaughtered other tribes. But nearly constant in what we can recover of the oldest strata of human culture is a sense that the world is an awesome, holy place – a place to be treated reverently, because it carries myriad wonderful mysteries.

With varying degrees of reflection, present-day people interested in reworking human consciousness, so as to make it compatible with the systems of the planet that many data now say are threatening to abort, can take up some version of the ancient cosmological myth.[2] They may draw on stories of ancient American Indians, or combine feminist instincts with a mythology of the pre-Christian European goddess, or follow threads of Indian non-violence (*ahimsa*) back to a Vedic sense of the sacredness of the earth. The sources for a remythologization of life are numerous, and many of them are very attractive. Bracketing the question of how to dismantle the engines of technology that have developed during the last centuries, people persuaded by ecological wisdom and wanting to imagine a radical reworking of human culture can yearn for older times, when the holiness of existence seemed more palpable. They can decry secularization, the flattening of human appreciation of the mysteries of creation, and so decry the technological if not scientific mentality that they descry behind secularization. Indeed, they can even tax the churches and synagogues with having forgotten their spiritual foundations: wonder at the great acts of God that made the world from nothingness and created a rational species able to appreciate it.

The advantages that a Christian faith is likely to find in such a movement to remythologize life are obvious enough. If new images, stories, rituals, or appreciations restore a sense of wonder at creation and veneration for creation's holy source, they can seem to be providing fuel to re-ignite a passionate appreciation of the biblical God. The disadvantages may be equally clear. Traditional Christian faith, developing seeds in the Bible, demythologized nature somewhat, insisting that only the sovereign Lord, Creator of heaven and earth, is truly holy, and that the sacrality of nature has severe limits. The biblical polemics against the divinities of the Canaanites stand as paradigmatic warnings. When added to a self-serving reading of Genesis 1.28, they tended to let human beings think that nature was their enemy, or at least their thrall, so that they could use the physical world just as they desired. That is the negative effect of the demythologizing of nature that Christian tradition often considered its birthright and obligation. The gospel held out a transcedent destiny for human beings, and if people remained immured in the cosmological myth they might miss it. God was offering not only the defeat of sin and death but the flowering of truly divine, eternal life. So the physical world, like human history, could appear to be of only limited and passing significance. In such a perspective, the remythologizing of life can seem to be a step backwards, into pagan unawareness of the reach of divine grace. What appeared in Jesus the Christ can seem so much more profound and precious than anything available in the cycles of physical nature that the two have little in common. Anything that even suggests that they are on a par, let alone that myths of nature are superior to the Christian myth, is deadly dangerous to the spiritual well-being of humankind. That is how theologians opposed to 'ecological wisdom' tend to reason, at least implicitly.

I shall deal in due course with the full programme of Christian praxis that an adequate response to the ecological crisis requires. For the moment, to complete these reflections on remythologization, let me indicate germs of a reworking of Christian mythology that might make the remythologization of life acceptable to the Christian orthodox. First, there is the story of creation, which makes it plain that everything in the universe came from God and is good in God's sight. Second, there is the Christian instinct that all of creation has occurred in the Word, which makes creation a function of the trinitarian processions and joins it to christology. Third, there is the love of matter that both God's original *fiat* and the incarnation of the Logos imply. Contrary to other mythologies that entered Christian culture, for orthodox faith matter is not the enemy of spirit, not the foe of either God or human beings. Fourth, there is the reconciliation of matter and spirit in sacramentality. The instinct that water is holy enough to be more than water, that bread and wine can signify beyond themselves similarly, depends on a faith that matter is a fit, even beautiful, vehicle for meaning. Meaning, which in its farthest reaches becomes revelation, has taken flesh and dwelt among us. It has blessed our bodies and habitats. Thus every human dwelling can seem like a shrine, a holy place. Thus any human act – work, play, eating, drinking, making love, mourning – can become a petition for God's help, a thanksgiving for God's bounty. We human beings cannot alienate the earth on which we stand, to which we return, because this earth is inseparable from our bodies. The story that the Christian good news has to provide, the myth needed in all times but especially sharply today, is that divine love, the source of creation and redemption, has warmed us from within. The world is ours to use as we see fit, but with a crucial qualification. The world is ours to use as we see fit when we live in wisdom of God's Word made flesh. For then we realize that everything that we have is gracious, and that our having it is a responsibility to cherish it and make it flourish.

III. Future Christian praxis

When we consider how a properly repristinated Christian myth might function to heed a proper 'ecological wisdom' and help human existence integrate itself better with the systems of the earth, we find ourselves drawn to such topics as a renewed Christian appreciation of creation, an application of Christian instincts about redemption to the physical world, a new reverence of God in the midst of physical creation, and a prophetic commitment to defend the rights of the natural environment. Let us contemplate these four topics.

First, a renewed Christian appreciation of creation could remind us that creation is ever-fresh, a continual grant of existence from the single and holy divine fount of being. For God to create cannot be separate from God's eternal being as a community of knowing and loving. Meister Eckhart was punished for his speculations along this line, but much of his instinct was sound: creation reposes in the endless mystery of the divine being itself. When we gaze out upon the lakes and steppes, we see beauty that has been prepared in eternity. Equally, we see beauty that is a presence of the perfection that the divine community of persons is and enjoys in the *tota simul* of its eternal bliss. The 'now' that blinds our eye and takes our breath away is a touch of the God who is always 'now'. Far from despising any creation, whether our own or that of 'lower' creatures, we Christians ought to write our own variations on the wonder that Leibnitz and Heidegger made foundational for philosophy: Why is there something rather than nothing? If there is something – even the lowly being of a mere rock – there is a grant of existence that is a sheer grace and so ought to be a great wonder to the religious mind. The more that Christians refresh their appreciation of the extraordinary character of creation, the more they will lay the foundations for a future ecological praxis that befits the world that God has given into our keeping. Far from taking for granted the planet on which we live, our contemplations of it ought to make us more religious, just as our religious works ought to make it more secure and prosperous.

Second, Christians would do well to extend their instincts about the redemption worked by Christ to the physical world. Among the neighbours wounded by sin, the planet now stands forth as an egregious example. And just as suffering raises in the truly Christian heart a profound compassion, reminiscent as such suffering is bound to be of the passion of Christ, so the present sufferings of physical nature ought to move Christians to a deep compassion. What is suffering from the pollutions caused by our current lifestyles is a fellow creature – a system of fellow creatures. Unless we are neighbour to this system of fellow creatures, our Lord is likely to disown us on Judgment Day. From people who press the cause of hapless animals, suffering from the incursions of human beings into their habitats, or from the diets of human beings, or from the experiments of human scientists, to people who lament the defacing of natural monuments or the littering of beaches, a great cast of sympathizers is ready to be assembled. In fact, the instinct to grieve for the devastations of the planet (human, animal, or subliving) is a natural extension of the Christian instinct to assimiliate all suffering beings to the crucified Christ. There is no stronger symbol of the depths to which God has gone to identify with our creaturely condition than the crucified Christ, and so there is no stronger focus for our hope that the divine love is always proving to be stronger than death. When we resurrect the dismal future of a planet apparently headed into irretrievable ecological ruin, we extend Christian hope to the full spectrum of God's creation, trusting that for all creatures, whales, and rare birds as well as starving children and sufferers from AIDS, God does promise to be all in all.

A third focus for a future Christian praxis responsive to the challenges put to us by God through the ecological crisis is a new reverence for the presence of God in physical creation. Christian faith has rightly stressed the wonders of the human person, created as an image of God. Apart from some extraordinary saints, such as Francis of Assisi, Christian faith has not been as aware of the divine presence in sub-human creation as it might have been. Other religious traditions – Hindu and Buddhist, Taoist and Shinto

– have been more sensitive to the sacrality of physical creation. We Christians would do well to listen to the inner impulse of geomancy, astrology, reverence of the Buddha-nature and the Tao. We could learn to hear better how God speaks in non-human voices. We could learn to pray in fresh negative accents. It is a thesis of Christian faith that we do not know what God is, and that whatever we say about God is more unlike than like what divinity is in itself. If our hearts expanded, became properly catholic, we might see that others have long preceded us in giving praise to the divinity manifested in the fall of the cherry blossom or the fertility of the cow. Certainly, we ought to criticize such praise in the light of the inter-personal communion that we believe the divine persons have established through the grace of Christ. But nothing need separate us from the love of our God in Christ Jesus, certainly nothing in the physical creation that our God has displayed for our wonder and use.

Last, the sufferings revealed in the current state of the earth make a strong claim on the prophetic responsibilities of people of biblical faith. If they know their sacred texts, Jews, Christians and Muslims can all read the current global signs of the times as a call for repentance, restitution and radical change. The 'poor of the Lord' now needing defence are not only the widows and orphans abandoned by a careless, affluent society. They are also the very systems of the natural world, from tide pools to rye grasses. Unless people of faith, people of unearthly commitments and loves, step forth to defend the most voiceless of God's creatures, great numbers of such creatures are going to perish, and much of the beauty of creation with them. This is a vast desecration, the sort that from time out of mind prophets have stridden forth to denounce. If Christians want an acute political agenda for the twentieth century, let them look to the very foundations of life itself. To defend these foundations will be very good work – something bound to bring into play both the imagery and the substance of the new Jerusalem.[3]

Notes

1. Any basic textbook in ecology supplies a wealth of information about current problems. See, for example, G. Tyler Miller, *Living in the Environment*, Belmont, California, updated regularly. See also the annual reports, *State of the World*, edited by Lester R. Brown for the Worldwatch Institute, New York.

2. On the cosmological myth, see Eric Voegelin, *Order and History*, Vol. 1, Baton Rouge, LA 1957. On religious mythology, see Denise Lardner Carmody and

John Carmody, *The Story of World Religions*, Mountain View, California 1988. I am grateful to my colleague Dr Mary Ann Hinsdale for information about ecofeminism.

3. For resources for Christian understanding and praxis, see Jürgen Moltmann, *God in Creation*, London and San Francisco 1985; H. Paul Santmire, *The Travail of Nature*, Philadelphia 1985; and Charles Birch et al. (eds.), *Liberating Life*, Maryknoll, NY 1990.

III · The Significance of the Biblical Vision of a 'New Heaven and a New Earth'

Responsibility for a 'New Heaven and a New Earth'

Roger Burggraeve

Reflection on ecology from a Christian standpoint cannot ignore the biblical category of 'new heaven and new earth' which we find in both the First Testament (cf. Isa. 66.2) and the Second (cf. Rev.21.1).[1]

I. Divine promise and human task

The expression 'heaven and earth', which refers directly to the first line of the Bible (Gen. 1.1), denotes the world, the cosmos, the universe. What Isaiah and John outline as a vision, we can also call the 'new world'. This idea opens up the perspective of a messianic or eschatological future, in which the cosmos is redeemed and perfected. This perfection may not just be understood as a restoration of today's 'broken world' to its original state, but is a transformation which surpasses all imagining based on the existing world: a perfecting as a 'new creation'.

Now this liberating and re-creating perfection of the world can be understood by itself: that is certainly not meaningless. In itself the cosmos is characterized not only by beauty and harmony but also by incompleteness, and above all by violence and destruction. However, in the biblical message, both in the First and the Second Testaments, 'the new heaven and the new earth' is usually spoken of only in the context of the 'new person' (cf. Ezek. 36.26; Rom. 5.14), in other words the redeemed and perfected person. One need only think of the story of the flood, where not only are human beings saved but the animals with them, and where the covenant between Yahweh and Noah also embraces nature: it is not only a covenant between Yahweh and the cosmos but also a covenant between human beings and nature (cf. Gen. 9.1–17). And in Isaiah's vision of messianic peace, of that time when the descendant of Jesse will secure justice for the weak and put an end to violence between human beings, the prophet also sees the removal of violence between the animals (Isa. 11.16) and throughout nature (Isa. 55.12). Nor is this an isolated idea, as is evident for example from Ezek. 34.24, 26–28; Joel 4.18. According to the prophets, the whole of creation looks to liberation from its suffering.

However, this is always combined with the idea of human liberation (cf. Isa. 60.19–20). This also applies to the Second Testament. Through the perspective of liberation and glorious restoration the Apocalypse seeks to comfort the new people of God in all their suffering and persecution. In order to implement this 'salvation-historical' perspective and give it a comprehensive significance, it is put in the context of a new heaven and a new earth, in which 'death will be no more; mourning and crying and pain will be no more, for the first things have passed away' (Rev. 21.4) Paul, too, speaks of the redemption of the cosmos in the context of human redemption: the whole of nature shares in the birthpangs which lead to the freedom of the children of God (Rom. 8.18–23). However, this does not mean that there is no mention in the Bible of the redemption and perfection of the earth in itself, but rather that there is no mention of the liberation and perfection of human beings as individuals and community (resurrection, the communion of saints) without also mention of the liberation of the cosmos. We could call this the radical anti-dualism of the biblical idea of redemption.

This link between salvation for human beings and salvation for the cosmos has some important implications for a correct understanding of the category of the new world. Thus this category presupposes that the present earth is not as it must be. In the biblical perspective this means that it is not just finite and fragile, but also shares in the 'sinfulness' of human beings, or rather, the Bible associates the fragility and aggression in it with the human history of evil and sin. The cosmos shares in human fate; it is marked by the consequences of sin, as emerges, for example, from the story of the flood, in which the harmony between human labour and nature (cf. Gen. 2.15) is fundamentally destroyed as a result of human sin (Gen. 3.17–19). Therefore the Bible understands the present state of nature in which non-human creatures often confront one another in a hostile way, giving rise to an inexorable struggle for life, not just as a 'natural' state of limitation consequential upon their createdness, but also and above all as a 'salvation-historical' state of unredeemedness.

In addition, it is clear that in scripture there is mention of perfection and 'new creation' only as redemption and liberation, in other words as a conquest of sin. This implies that the idea of perfection is not just a theological idea of divine promise and grace, but also has an essential ethical dimension. The idea of a new world means not only that the present world is not as it must be, but also and above all that this is a result of human sin. The promise of a new world is consequently not just a promise for a 'remote' or ultimate future which we shall receive gratis – in superabundant grace – from God, but at the same time means a radical questioning of our present relationship with the world. In this respect the promise of the new world also contains an urgent ethical task, the need to be aware of our sinful relationship to the world, to be converted and – in the power of the promise – even now to work on the new world held in prospect for us. In this way human beings are also 'the mediators of redemption, the indispensable stage of the movement which starts from God'.[2]

In order to understand in what sense we can now already prepare for this 'new creation', we need to return to the 'first creation', in other words to the world and our relationship to this world as it was originally meant by God. The biblical fact of creation does not just have a protological significance; it also has an eschatological significance. As a pointer towards the beginning, at the same time it opens up perspectives on what is the 'desirable' relationship between human beings and the world (and on what this relationship certainly may *not* be), in other words on a relationship which corresponds 'as far as possible' to the vision of the new world.

In order to get some idea of the implications of the 'first creation' for the 'new creation' as an ethical orientation, I have opted for a philosophical reading in depth of the biblical account of creation, above all of Genesis 1.[3] Such a philosophical reading begins from the fact that anthropological, metaphysical, ontological and ethical views are implied in scripture which can be made explicit in such a way that they can be reflected on and communicated.[4]

II. Our creaturely responsibility for the world

We could also call the book of Genesis, or the 'Book of the Origin', the book of the 'Origin before the Origin'. It is about the creation of human beings by God, in other words about the origin which precedes human beings as an origin and beginning. The biblical affirmation that human beings are created implies that they are not their own origin: they are not in any way *causa sui* (the cause of themselves). Something has already happened to me before I can make myself happen. This 'primal passivity' reveals my created condition as a human being: I am created, and this createdness consitutes my 'basic condition'.[5] I shall now develop the implications of this.

First of all we note how human beings are the last to be created: according to Genesis 1 they are created only on the vigil of the sabbath.[6] They are the last to come into the world, the 'special reserve' of creation. So this world is not what human beings have themselves wanted and developed. The world itself is not something of which human beings have seen the beginning: it precedes them by five full days. Human beings did not sprout from human creative freedom and imagination. They are placed in a world which was already completely there.[7] The world is first encountered by human beings (with the emphasis on the passive form of the verb, 'is'), and only after that is it worked on. The world is the past of, or rather for, human beings.[8]

Moreover, the world itself is also created; it comes forth from the sovereign word of God. And as 'created' it belongs to God and not to human beings, who themselves are also creatures. So the world is not in any way human *property*. As a creation it is *given* to human beings. Human beings must 'get' and 'receive' the world: they have no fundamental right to it. The world is not just a factual given that human beings encounter, but in the literal meaning of the word it is a 'given' that can only belong to human beings if it is 'given' to them. This means that if human beings 'take' and 'appropriate' the earth, they are usurpers and robbers. They have no right or privilege; rather, they are the 'last to come'. Those who possess and work the earth as though it belonged to them act as if it came about 'through them'. This leads them into untruth: they forget their created-ness, or rather they give themselves the illusion of 'uncreatedness'.[9]

However, this is not yet the whole story of the creaturely relationship of human beings to the world. A further philosophical deepening of the biblical fact of creation demonstrates how from the beginning this relationship is of a strictly ethical kind, not on the basis of a free human choice but as 'created' by God himself. Human beings are not just put in the world as a 'being among other beings', but created in an ethical relationship to the world: they discover that they stand in an 'ethical bond' with creation.

We can distinguish various aspects of this ethical mode of being which men and women have towards the world. First of all we can indicate *formally* the ethical bond between human beings and the world. According to Genesis 1.26, 28 the world is not just given to human beings: they have to do something with it, namely 'subject' it and 'rule' it. The Jewish

Talmud expresses this in an evocative way by explaining that although human beings were the lastcomers of creation, they were the first to be punished. They are made responsible for creation. And if creation is perverted, then they are the first to be held accountable.[10]

We need to understand this accountability properly. It is not a responsibility which arises out of human freedom and free choice, but a 'creaturely responsibility', in other words a responsibility which is given with one's very createdness and which thus precedes one's freedom. In current Western thought human responsibility is defined on the basis of human subjecthood. The fact that men and women are responsible beings rests on the fact that they define and proclaim themselves as a self, which as 'self-awareness' is the origin, the *arche* or principle, beginning and end, alpha and omega, of their own thought, judgment, action and giving of meaning.[11]

However, quite a different concept of responsibility emerges from the biblical fact of creation, namely a responsibility which is constitutive of our very createdness. As 'created', this responsibility is also 'pre-original' and 'an-archic'. These terms need to be taken literally. Human responsibility for creation does not have its beginning and origin in human subjectivity as the origin and beginning (*arche*) of human actions. Our humanity consists precisely in being called to account 'despite ourselves', in other words even before we assume ourselves as a calling or choose a calling by ourselves. From this it becomes evident how the 'primal passivity' of our condition of creation is an ethical primal passivity.

This implies a radical redefining of human subjectivity. The biblical view of our createdness implies an ethical definition of humanity, namely that our creaturely responsibility is the first and fundamental 'nature' of subjectivity. This means that responsibility is not a simply *attribute* of subjectivity, as if it first existed intrinsically before the ethical relationship of involvement in other than oneself, viz. the world. Here the ethical does not appear as a supplement which is only added subsequently to a preceding neutral basis of being or substance. It is in the ethical self, understood as 'being made responsible', that the 'rub', the pain of subjectivity lies. According to the biblical account of creation, subjectivity is not something *per se*; from the beginning it is something for others. Our humanity is fundamentally a matter of 'being directed to others than ourselves', viz. to the world, that we have not in any way opted for, but for which we are made inescapably responsible. This responsibility is a form of 'commitment', or rather of 'being committed despite oneself'. We are without more ado that commitment; it is our created 'ethical mode' or way of being. We can also call it our 'ethical creatureliness'.[12]

Now if we look at the content of this creaturely responsibility, we can see how heteronomous it is: from elsewhere and through Someone else. God has created human beings as an ethical sense and direction: we have been inspired (literally 'inblown') and animated (literally 'ensouled') ethically by God.

In addition, my ethical creatureliness directs me to what I myself have not done. I have been made responsible for something of which I was never the author. I must give an account of something that I myself did not will and that is not born of my creativity (imagination, sketching, planning). I have to make myself responsible over and above my capacity for freedom, as it were outside the sphere of the openness to accountability which expresses the 'measure' of my freedom. I am essentially 'involved in the other (the world)', and am so before my inspection, claim or dialogue which comes from me.[13]

In other words, we are put in an ethically demanding 'bond' with others than ourselves, the world. This completely heteronomous responsibility in which we are created is, moreover, sheer *solidarity*, but not solidarity which arises from our own free choice, and thus from our capacity or ability. It is a solidarity which is 'done to me' and puts me in an inescapable position of responsibility towards the world despite myself. This ethical solidarity is a creaturely solidarity in the strict sense of the word, precisely because it has its origin in a radical passivity: I have come to be, or rather am coming to be – created by God – in solidarity with what I myself have not made, which I could not even make because it was not yet there. So this is a solidarity which lies hidden from time immemorial or in a 'time before my time'.[14] We can also call this creaturely solidarity a kind of 'fate' which already 'grips' me and gives me ethical orientation even before I can grasp anything or give myself an ethical orientation. I am already bound up with the world even before I can resolve whether or not to adopt a responsible attitude to the world and thus to live in 'a state of understanding'. I am committed to the fate of the world without being asked and without willing it, so that I can no longer say that the world is not my concern.

The question now is how we need to understand this creaturely responsibility towards the world. In other words, what is the perspective and aim of ruling over the world? To discover this we need to go deeper into the concept of creation itself in Genesis 1.

From the first verses of Genesis 1 it emerges how God did not just create. We usually think of the act of creation in an ontological, neutral way, namely as putting into existence a multiplicity of juxtaposed entities which once were not there. However, creation is more than this creation of entities 'from nothing'. God did not create without being concerned about the direction and sense of creation. He put a significant *telos* in all that is created. Moreover, that at the beginning – when God created heaven and earth – 'the earth was without form and void, and darkness lay upon the earth' (Gen. 1.1–2) is not just a so-called mythological remnant. The divine creation is precisely creation of an order from the chaos of the *tohuwabohu*, in other words, bringing a sense and direction through 'light'. Hence creation also runs an ordered course by days and achieves itself dynamically by a rising line of the division and distinction of 'creatures' up as far as human beings.[15] And with the coming of human beings, the 'order' or 'meaning' has a direct ethical interpretation: the sense of creation is an ethical sense, namely the responsibility of human beings for creation as an 'image of God' (Gen. 1.27), in other words as 'representatives' of God and thus as God wills it.

But what is the 'meaning' or goal of creation which is also created by God? In accord with the whole development of the Old Testament revelation, rabbinc literature gives us an interesting and important indication of this. There, according to a midrash, the sixth day of creation is also the day on which the Torah is given to Israel: the meaning of creation and the task of human beings lies in realizing the Torah. The world was created so that Israel could carry out the Torah, in other words so that the ethical order of 'doing righteousness' should have a possibility of being realized, not only in connection with fellow human beings but also in connection with the world itself.[16]

If we want to formulate this significance of creation in terms of the wider, global perspective of the whole Bible, we can say that the 'purpose' which God has laid down in his creation, not as a natural law but as a task for humankind, is the messianic future of *shalom*, on which the new covenant embracing the world rests, and in which nature too is involved, as is increasingly clearly indicated by the prophets. It emerges from the New Testament how Jesus sees the significance of creation in this perspective as the coming and realization of the kingdom of God, in other words as the promise and the praxis of God's liberating preferential love for the poor, those who weep, those who are in need and are persecuted, both personally and in community.[17] And both in Paul (Rom. 8.19–22) and in Revelation (21.1) it is evident that the final realization of the kingdom of God also implies a 'new creation', in other words the redemption and consummation of the cosmos.

III. Western autonomous thought put in question

This ethically qualified creaturely relationship between human beings and the world leads us to formulate a radical criticism of Western autonomous thought, which often functions in a one-sided way, positing human beings as an *arche* and 'principle' which has control over everything.

Anyone who interprets the human subject as the centre of the world and as the measure of all things will involuntarily attribute all power and 'right' over the world to human beings, or rather think spontaneously that the world is the exclusive 'domain' and 'possession' of human beings, so that they can exercise their right of freedom there. Anyone who thinks of human beings as the *arche*, the principle, will think of everything else as 'secondary', as it were purely as a function of human beings and as arising from human beings. This functionalistic and instrumentalistic anthropocentrism has produced and determined all current Western reflection and praxis about possessions and the tyrannical exploitation of the world.

In an extreme way this absolutist manner of thinking of the world in terms of possessions and power has become clear in the way in which Western industry and the technological consumer society treats animals. This accusation has rightly been made by, among others, Peter Singer, the pioneer of the 'New Animal Liberation Movement'.[18] In many respects present-day human beings have totally reified animals, as it were reduced them to a pure object, function and means.[19] An evocative illustration of this is bio-industry with its 'animal factories',[20] in which animals are simply 'bio-machines on hoofs'.[21] It is the story of their artificially disrupted rhythm of days and years, their unnatural living space which is reduced to an absolute minimum, without 'social intercourse' with other animals, or in which the social milieu is so limited that they are led to excessive aggression and to cannibalism. The 'intelligent' breeder of course adapts the animal to the production system by all kinds of interventions, sedatives and medicines, with the aim of increasing production and being able to hold his own against the spiral of an inexorable competitive struggle on the macro-scale.[22] We also see an analogous reification of animals in the exploitation of laboratory animals.[23] Never before have 'developed' human beings regarded animals so much in reified functional terms as mere *objects* for all kinds of scientific research, which can be thrown away after they have been used.[24] It should also be noted that animals are not just used for medical research, but for military research, for the cosmetics and detergent industry, for space travel, psychological and behavioural research, the testing of weedkillers and insecticides, and so on.[25] Scientific language itself also illustrates how animals have become part of an objective scientific system. The researcher does not need an 'animal' but a 'model'. While investigating and manipulating the 'model', researcher may easily forget that they are really dealing with living beings.[26]

This functionalistic reduction of animals has not just been conjured up out of thin air. It is deeply rooted in the whole of Western culture, and in a special way in what we have begun to call 'modernity', of which Descartes was one of the pioneers. In Descartes we meet the so-called 'apartheid view' in the most extreme form. He posited a total break between human beings and animals. For him the animal has completely become a thing, which amounts to an 'absolute repudiation'.[27] Like the human body, so too animals – as corporeal beings without reason – are just machines, 'automata', which cannot think and feel. The practical consequences of this theory were disastrous. On the basis of it people thought it justified, for example, to nail down living dogs unanaesthetized and then cut them open to study their anatomy and muscular systems. No notice was to be taken of their cries: machines make a racket, but they do not feel.[28]

However, this Cartesian total reduction of the animal to an object is not a chance whim but an expression of Cartesian rationalism and thus of the rise of 'modernity'. Here the human subject and its autonomy is central, and this has become established in an extremely functional and instrumental approach to nature. The world is no longer experienced as 'creation' but as an 'object' of human knowledge and ability. The men of the Enlightenment began to approach reality increasingly as being at their disposal, from the human project of existence in autonomous freedom. The result of this was that everything else derived its significance from the fact that it could and should make a contribution to human self-determination, both individual and social. This slowly but surely ended up in the present-day Western instrumentalistic anthropocentrism, which as rational, strategic and economic thought in terms of usefulness and efficiency reduced everything else to a means to be used in the self's emancipatory struggle for identity.[29]

According to Singer, however, the remote roots of this instrumental anthropocentrism, and of the reification of animals in particular, lie in the Jewish view of creation.[30] He is not alone in this view, nor was he in any way the first to hold it.[31] As early as 1967, L. White pointed to Western Christianity as the root of the modern way of dealing with nature and its destruction of the environment.[32] According to C. Amery (1974), the fatal origin of the typically Christian myth of growth which devastates the environment lies in Gen. 1.28.[33] In his view this verse produced a pernicious gulf between human beings and other beings, and put human beings in an almost divine position, which involuntarily gave them control over non-human beings. Therefore according to L. Lemaire, a 'turning to the Earth, as the one true dwelling place for human beings and all other living beings, must free itself from the Christian tradition'.[34]

We cannot deny that the fundamental desacralization of nature by Jewish-Christian monotheism has made an important contribution to the formation of science and technology. That human beings are called on to subject the earth, to work it and rule over it, implies that human beings are not subject to nature. The Bible disenchants nature, which as an untameable and numinous superior power has human beings in its grasp, terrifies and fascinates them. Through belief in creation, human beings are made free to deal with the world in a matter-of-fact and rational way. However, that in itself does not mean that one can unconditionally derive the destructive approach to nature associated with present-day industrial society from the biblical creation-monotheism which exalts human beings to co-creators, and identify such an approach with it. Nevertheless, it cannot be denied that Western Christians in the past (above all since the rise of bourgeois capitalism) have interpreted Genesis 1.26, 28 in a one-sidedly activist and instrumentalist way, precisely in order to legitimate the exploitation of nature. However, the real question is whether this interpretation is inherent in the biblical view of human beings. Or rather, it is clear from the idea of creatureliness, which is implied in the biblical account of creation, that such an interpretation is completely opposed to this. It seems, rather, that Western Christianity – above all in modern times – has compromised itself all too readily, because of an apologetic, insufficiently critical concern to 'keep up with the times', with the ideology of freedom, progress and domination which slowly but surely established itself in the West on the basis of the so-called anthropocentric shift from the seventeenth century onwards, and subsequently infiltrated itself all over the world by all kinds of colonialism and domination.

IV. Conclusion

At all events, one-sided Western autonomous thought, which reduces the cosmos to a pure instrument and function of self-glorifying human arbitrariness, is completely opposed to the idea of the 'new creation'; even more, it makes 'the new heaven and the new earth' impossible. Therefore this autonomous thought must be radically unmasked and put in question as 'sin' ('the sin of the West'). According to the biblical idea of creation, human beings may not do what they want with the world, in the service of their own individual plans for existence, directed towards their own fulfilment. In other words, they must not just do something with the world, but they must do something definite with it. They are given a specific task, and this also implies that they must give an account to God. They must develop themselves in the direction of 'the new heaven and the new earth', as the milieu for the realization and the coming of God's kingdom of peace and righteousness.

Translated by John Bowden

Notes

1. Cf. C. Chalier, *L'Alliance avec la nature*, Paris 1989, 138–207.
2. E. Levinas, *Hors sujet*, Montpellier 1987, 85: 'l'homme est le médiateur de la rédemption, indispensable relais du mouvement que part de Dieu.'
3. This is certainly not the only valid way. Moltmann, for example, argues for an ecological theology not only from God as transcendent creator but also from the immanent Spirit and the eschatological messiah; he also calls this a trinitarian and messianic doctrine of creation. Cf. J. Moltmann, *God in Creation. An Ecological Doctrine of Creation*, London and San Francisco 1985.
4. E. Levinas, *Quatre lectures talmudiques*, Paris 1968, 119.
5. Id., *Autrement qu'être ou au-delà de l'essence*, The Hague 1974, 71.
6. Id., *Du sacré au saint. Cinq nouvelles lectures talmudiques*, Paris 1977, 123.
7. Ibid., 136.
8. Id., *Quatre lectures talmudiques* (n.4), 136.
9. Id., *En découvrant l'existence avec Husserl et Heidegger*, Paris 1967, 176.
10. Id., *Quatre lectures talmudiques* (n.4), 136.
11. Id., *De Dieu qui vient à l'idée*, Paris 1982, 97–104.
12. Id., *Éthique et Infini. Dialogues avec Philippe Nemo*, Paris 1982, 101–3.
13. Id., *Autrement qu'être ou au-delà de l'essence* (n.5), 71.
14. Id., *Humanisme de l'autre homme*, Montpellier 1972, 78.
15. Cf. R. Burggraeve, *Zin-volle seksualiteit*, Louvain 1985, 63–75.
16. Id., *Quatre lectures talmudiques* (n.4), 90.
17. Cf. R. Burggraeve, 'Responsibility Precedes Freedom: In Search of a Personalistic Love Ethic', in J. Selling (ed.), *Personalist Morals. Essays in Honor of Professor Louis Janssens*, Louvain 1988, 113–20.
18. P. Singer, *Animal Liberation*, New York 1975.
19. E.Doornenbal, 'Dierenproeven en hun consequenties', in H. Smid (ed.), *Dierproeven in de moderne samenleving*, 1978, 197f.
20. Cf. J. Mason and P. Singer, *Animal Factories*, New York 1980.
21. For an illustration see the following quotation from a specialist journal for pig-breeders in the Netherlands, quoted by U. Melle, *Menselijke en andere dieren*, in S. Ijsseling (ed.), *Over de mens. Vijf filosofische conferenties*, Louvain 1987, 85–7: 'We

must forget that a pig is an animal. Regard it as a machine in a factory which also needs a drop of oil from time to time. The casting of piglets must be regarded as the start of a conveyer belt. And the cattle trade as the delivery of end-products.'

22. R. R. Harrison, 'Ethical Questions concerning Modern Livestock Farming', in D. Petterson and R. D. Ryder (eds.), *Animals' Rights. A Symposium*, Sussex and London 1970, 122–30.

23. Smid (ed.), *Dierproeven* (n.19); A. Elsaesser, 'Lassen sich Tierversuche ethisch rechtfertigen?', in *Stimmen der Zeit* 11, 1986, 732–6.

24. H. van Praag, 'Ten Geleide', in Smit (ed.), *Dierproeven* (n.19), 13.

25. R. D. Ryder, 'Psychologische experimenten met dieren', in Smid (ed.), *Dierproeven* (n.19), 208–9.

26. B. E. Rollin, *Animal Rights and Human Morality*, Buffalo, NY, 110–11.

27. B. Midgley, *Animals and Why They Matter. A Journey around the Species Barrier*, Aylesbury 1983, 45f.

28. Cf. T. Regan and P. Singer (eds.), *Animal Rights and Human Obligations*, Engelwood Cliffs 1976, 435.

29. A. Auer, *Umweltethik. Ein theologischer Beitrag zur ökologischen Diskussion*, Düsseldorf 1985, 19f.; G. Noller, 'Die ökologische Herausforderung an die Theologie', *Evangelische Theologie* 34, 1974, 592.

30. Singer, *Animal Liberation* (n.18), 25–30.

31. Cf. G. Manenschijn, *Geplunderde aarde, getergde hemel. Ontwerp voor een christlijke milieu-ethiek*, Baarn 1988, 78–85.

32. L. White, 'The Historical Roots of our Ecological Crisis', *Science* 155, 1967, 1203–7. In a later article he refines his thesis and develops it further: id., 'The Historical Roots of our Ecological Crisis. Continuing the Conversation', in H. G. Barbour, *Western Man and Environmental Ethics. Attitudes towards Nature and Technology*, 1973, 18–30.

33. C. Amery, *Das Ende der Vorsehung. Die gnadenlosen Folgen des Christentums*, Reinbek 1974.

34. T. Lemaire, 'Een nieuwe aarde. Utopie en ecologie', in W. Achterberg and W.Zweers (eds.), *Milieufilosofie tussen theorie en praktijk*, Utrecht 1986, 285.

Contributors

JOHAN DE TAVERNIER was born in 1957 and gained his doctorate in moral theology in 1988 with a thesis on 'The Human Reality of Experience and the Christian Experience of Reality. Ethically Relevant Experiences and the Theological Foundations for a Social Ethic with a Christian Inspiration'. Since 1990 he has been an assistant in the faculty of religion at the Catholic University of Louvain. He also works at the Centre for Peace Theology. He has written articles on faith and ethics and on various issues in social ethics.

RENÉ COSTE, a priest of Saint-Sulpice, was born in 1922. He is Professor of Social Theology at the Theological Faculty of the Catholic Institute of Toulouse, and Ecclesiastical Delegate General of Pax Christi, France. He has taught in several universities in Europe and Canada, and is consultant to the Pontifical Council for Dialogue with Non-Believers. His twenty-eight books include *Le problème du droit de guerre dans la pensée de Pie XII* (1962); *Morale internationale* (1964); *Théologie de la liberté religieuse* (1969); *Analyse marxiste et foi chrétienne* (1976); *Le devenir de l'homme (Projet marxiste, Projet chrétien)*)1979); *L'amour qui change le monde (Theologie de la charité)* (1981); *Le grand secret des Béatitudes* (1985); and *L'Église et les défis du monde* (1986). He has written more than 200 articles in reviews and joint works, and about 1500 newspaper articles.

ANTON VAN HARSKAMP was born at Oosterbeek, The Netherlands, in 1946. He gained his doctorate at the Catholic University of Nijmegen. He is now associated with the Interdisciplinary Centre for the Study of Science, Society and Religion of the Free University of Amsterdam. He has written articles on ideological criticism in theology, Catholic theology in the nineteenth century and the relationship between theology and the social sciences.

ALEXANDRE GANOCZY was born in Budapest in 1928 and studied at the Pazmany University there, at the Institute Catholique in Paris, and the Pontifical Gregorian University in Rome. A doctor of theology and philosophy, he is Professor of Systematic Theology in the University of Würzburg. He has written various articles and several books, including *Le jeune Calvin*, Wiesbaden 1966; *Ecclesia ministrans*, Freiburg im Breisgau 1968; *Sprechen von Gott in heutiger Gesellschaft*, Freiburg im Breisgau 1974; *Der schöpferische Mensch und die Schöpfung Gottes*, Mainz 1976; *Einführung in die Dogmatik*, Darmstadt 1983; *Einführung in die katholische Sakramentenlehre*, Darmstadt ²1984; *Dieu grace pour le monde*, Paris 1986; *Schöpfungslehre*, Düsseldorf ²1987; *Aus seiner Fülle haben wir alle empfangen. Grundriss der Gnadenlehre*, Düsseldorf 1989.

GÜNTER ALTNER was born in 1936; he is a doctor of science and a doctor of theology. Between 1971 and 1973 he was Professor of Human Biology in the Pädagogische Hochschule of Schwäbisch-Gmünd, and from 1977 he has been Professor of Theology in the University of Koblenz-Landau; he is also a member of the board of the Eco-Institute of Freiburg im Breisgau. He has written numerous works on the interface between science and theology and the problems of assessing the consequences of technology, most recently *Die Überlebenskrise in der Gegenwart – Ansätze zum Dialog mit der Natur in Naturwissenschaft und Theologie*, Darmstadt 1987.

JOHAN VAN KLINKEN works as a physicist at the Dutch Foundation for Fundamental Research on Matter. He obtained his PhD in 1965 at the University of Groningen, The Netherlands, on experiments with polarized electrons. His investigations into 'broken symmetries' touch on the origin of matter and life. In addition to his research he is involved in nature conservation and ecology and in ecumenical and Pugwash studies of peace issues. His *Het Derde Punt*, Kampen 1989, was written as a contribution to the conciliar process from a scientific background.

WERNER KROH was born in Papenburg in 1949. He studied in St Georgen, Frankfurt am Main, and Münster, where at present he is engaged in research to qualify as a university teacher. He worked as assistant to J. B. Metz from 1980 to 1982, gaining his doctorate in 1982; from 1984 to 1987 he was a chaplain in Hanover. In addition to a number of articles he has written *Kirche im gesellschaftlichen Widerspruch. Zur*

Verständigung zwischen katholischer Soziallehre und politischer Theologie, Munich 1982.

JOHN CARMODY was born in Worcester, MA, in 1939 and gained his doctorate from Stanford University. At present he is senior research fellow at the University of Tulsa, Oklahoma. His more than forty books include *Ecology and Religion*, New York 1983, and *Religion: The Great Questions*, New York 1983.

ROGER BURGGRAEVE was born in Passendale, Belgium, in 1942; he studied philosophy in Rome at the Papal Salesian University and moral theology in Louvain, where since 1988 he has been Professor of Moral Theology at the Catholic University. He is founder and President of the Centre for Peace Theology. His publications include *Het gelaat van de bevrijding. Een heilsdenken in het spoor van Emmanuel Levinas*, Tielt 1986; *Emmanuel Levinas. Une bibliographie primaire et secondaire (1929–1989)*, Louvain 1990; *Levinas over vrede en mensenrechten*, Louvain 1990, and numerous articles on the ethics of peace, sexual ethics, faith and ethics, ethical methodology, ethics and education, and the thought of Levinas.

Members of the Advisory Committee for Dogma

Directors

Johann-Baptist Metz	Münster	Germany
Edward Schillebeeckx OP	Nijmegen	The Netherlands

Members

Rogério de Almeida Cunha	S. Joãa del Rei MG	Brazil
Ignace Berten OP	Rixensart	Belgium
Clodovis Boff	Rio de Janeiro	Brazil
Leonardo Boff OFM	Petrópolis	Brazil
Anne Carr	Chicago, Ill.	USA
Fernando Castillo	Santiago	Chile
Marie-Dominique Chenu OP	Paris	France
Yves Congar OP	Paris	France
Karl Derksen OP	Utrecht	The Netherlands
Severino Dianich	Caprona/Pisa	Italy
Josef Doré	Paris	France
Bernard-Dominique Dupuy	Paris	France
Donal Flanagan	Maynooth	Ireland
José González-Faus	Barcelona	Spain
Hermann Häring	Nijmegen	The Netherlands
Anton Houtepen	Utrecht	The Netherlands
Elizabeth Johnson CSJ	Washington, DC	USA
Joseph Komonchak	Washington, DC	USA
Nicholas Lash	Cambridge	England
René Laurentin	Evry-Cedex	France
Karl Lehmann	Mainz	Germany
James McCue	Iowa City, Iowa	USA
Carlo Molari	Rome	Italy
Heribert Mühlen	Paderborn	Germany
Peter Nemeshegyi SJ	Tokyo	Japan
Herwi Rikhof	Nijmegen	The Netherlands
Josef Rovira Belloso	Barcelona	Spain
Luigi Sartori	Padua	Italy
Piet Schoonenberg SJ	Nijmegen	The Netherlands
Robert Schreiter CPpS	Chicago, Ill.	USA
Dorothee Sölle	Hamburg	Germany
Jean-Marie Tillard OP	Ottawa/Ont.	Canada
Tharcisse Tshibangu Tshishiku	Kinshasa	Zaire
Herbert Vorgrimler	Münster	Germany
Bonifac Willems OP	Nijmegen	The Netherlands

Members of the Board of Directors

Issues of Concilium to be published in 1992:

Towards the African Synod
edited by G. Alberigo and A. Ngindu Mushete
The African church speaks out on the occasion of the holding of an African Synod to make Christians on other continents aware of its significance.
1992/1 February

The New Europe - A Challenge for Christians
edited by N. Greinacher and N. Mette
Deals with the vital questions raised by a new, united Europe: its role in world peace; the place of ecumenism; and the need for a new model for the church.
1992/2 April

Fundamentalism in the World's Religions
edited by Hans Küng and Jürgen Moltmann
Examines the problems fundamentalism creates for ecumenism between Judaism, Islam and Christianity, and searches for answers to those problems.
1992/3 June

God, Where are you? A Cry in the Night
edited by Christian Duquoc and Casiano Floristán
A discussion of the silence of God and the ways in which it is manifested: as sickness, death, exploitation, and God's inaccessibility to the sinner.
1992/4 August

The Tabu of Democracy in the Church
1992/5 October

The Debate on Modernity
1992/6 December

And for 1993:

1993/1 **Messianism in History**
1993/2 **The Spectre of Mass Death**
1993/3 **Mass Media**
1993/4 **Resurrection or Reincarnation?**
1993/5 **Migrants and Refugees: The Moral Challenge**
1993/6 **Christ in Asia?**